5/99

6/99

GAYLORD MG

INSIDE THE NRA

ARMED AND DANGEROUS

An Exposé

INSIDE THE NRA

ARMED AND DANGEROUS

An Exposé

By Jack Anderson

DOVE
BOOKS

ISBN 0-7871-0677-1

Printed in the United States of America

Dove Books
301 North Cañon Drive
Beverly Hills, CA 90210

Distributed by Penguin USA

Text design and layout by Carolyn Wendt
Jacket design and layout by Rick Penn-Kraus
Jacket illustration by Dean Kennedy

First Printing: January 1996

10 9 8 7 6 5 4 3 2 1

*This work is dedicated in all sincerity
to members of the National Rifle Association,
at least the moderate majority,
who deserve to know where their leaders stand
and how they are spending the membership dues.*

CONTENTS

ACKNOWLEDGMENTS

I have survived forty-nine years of Washington combat—of shooting and being shot at. Since the National Rifle Association uses real guns, I am pleased to share the honor with a band of dedicated associates, who operate in Washington somewhat like a political M*A*S*H unit.

There are three names I should single out: my daughter, Laurie Anderson-Bruch, who headed the research team; William Harrington, who brought order to three huge boxes full of documentation; and Daryl Gibson Smith, the former editor of my column, who applied the spit-and-polish.

PROLOGUE

I was a naive tenderfoot reporter when I was let loose on the nation's capital nearly half a century ago. My mores had been formed while growing up in an austere Mormon family, and so the exposure to political Washington was something of a cultural shock.

I joined the staff of the late Drew Pearson, a crusading columnist who battled for humanitarian causes and assailed racists and rascals in both public and corporate life. He viewed them as subverters of the American system and exploiters of the underprivileged.

Drew took infinite pains to impress upon me the moral objectives of the newspaper column and the just society: to champion the cause of the voiceless instead of the dominant, the dissenter as well as the organization, the helpless against their exploiters, the small enterprise over the octopus, the public's right to know and control rather than the official's prerogative to conceal and manipulate.

Drew's view of the larger role of the media has been vindicated in the decades since his death by the growth of investigative, muckraking reporting. The *Columbia Journalism Review*, the holy writ of journalism, has dubbed me the "King of the Muckrakers." Drew would have been pleased.

It is my peculiar function, as a confessed muckraker, to uncover what the government covers up. Unfortunately, I've become all too successful at detecting scandals in the dark corners of government. The antisocial proclivities of our politicians can be counted on to keep me occupied.

Yet this has never shaken my belief in the basic foundations of the American system. I have always regarded myself as part of the system, not as an alienated critic. For every rogue I've exposed there has always been a politician who battled for the public good.

In an age when so many things are wrong with America, people may have begun to doubt even those things that are right. American values have been impaired by a deepening sense of gloom—by accusation and denial, alarm and mistrust, duplicity and uncertainty.

I've contributed to the national pessimism, I suppose, by exposing wrongdoing in high places. Yet I emphatically disagree with those who see us as fallen leaves in the river of history, being swept downstream by a swift, irreversible tide. America is still founded on sound, fundamental principles, and fundamental verities are changeless.

Perhaps we should try to see this country through the eyes of an outsider—such as those of a British hiker named Stephen Fern, who described his view of America from a peak high atop the Rocky Mountains: "Strange to say, I began to cry. Sometimes

4

the sheer scale of America overwhelmed me. I sniffed, frowned, and wiped a sleeve across my cheek."

Or listen to the words of French actor Yves Montand: "You want to criticize America? *Bien.* America is not perfect. But be careful when you criticize America's political institutions. They are the safeguard of freedom on this planet."

Most of our forebears came here to escape political or economic oppression. They took a deep breath of freedom, rolled up their sleeves, and went to work. They cleared the wilderness; they farmed the land; they built our cities.

The taming of the West had been accomplished before I was born. But the rugged frontier spirit still lingered. Men still packed guns in their pickup trucks; boys were still taught how to shoot a gun before they learned how to drive a car.

One of my early recollections is of a showdown over water rights. It happened in Idaho farming country, where a passel of my cousins lived. I had been shipped there, at age eight, for a summer of riding, roping, and farm chores. The water dispute, I remember, got ugly. It didn't occur to the disputants to hire lawyers and file lawsuits. They loaded their guns and rode off on horseback to claim the water hole. Hours later, my cousins reappeared in gruff triumph; the other side had backed down after a long standoff.

I found journalism less grueling than farmwork and landed my first reporting job at age twelve. I covered the small town of Murray, Utah, for a weekly newspaper whose publisher was more interested in advertising than editorial content.

In my early twenties, I became a war correspondent. Well, not exactly. I persuaded a Salt Lake City paper, the *Deseret*

News, to arrange my accreditation in return for stories about hometown heroes gone off to World War II. But I promoted that fragile accreditation as though it had the full backing of the *New York Times.*

I immediately forgot about Utah's heroes for a chance to write about Chinese guerrillas operating behind Japanese lines. I arranged to be dropped off with some smuggled supplies deep inside China, where I wandered about with a guerrilla band. Deep though we were behind enemy lines, I covered only one skirmish—not against the Japanese enemy, but rather against a rival Chinese group. Nevertheless, I rode in splendid triumph through the rice paddies aboard the guerrilla troop's lone horse, which they had captured earlier from the Japanese. Unhappily, it was still loyal to the Japanese cause and inflicted my only war wound: a kick in the back.

I have recounted my background briefly so that you may know where I'm coming from. For I have written a book that will incite stout resistance. It's an inside account of the National Rifle Association, which has cast a long shadow over Washington. You are entitled to discern from my past whether I might have undertaken this assignment with malice or prejudice.

I will say only this in my own defense: I am a veteran of Washington combat. I've had a turbulent career of exposing villainies and being despised for it. Still, I've always let the shrapnel fall where it may. My style is simple and straightforward.

So, to quote the late Lyndon Johnson, "Let's lift up the cow's tail and look the situation straight in the face."

CHAPTER ONE
THE NRA:
THEN AND NOW

In most of the years I spent in Washington, I remained unfazed by reports of the city's rising crime rate. I automatically avoided certain neighborhoods, told my nine children to do the same, and then went about my life unafraid. We never locked the front door of our house. Our children and grandchildren and their friends flowed so freely through that door it would have been impractical to issue enough keys to keep it locked. I think that if a burglar had passed by our bed in the dark of night, my wife, Olivia, would have gotten up to get him a drink of water or taken him by the hand and led him to the bathroom.

If I had cause to look over my shoulder when I walked the streets of the nation's capital, it was only because I was accustomed to being tailed by the CIA or FBI agents on assignment from paranoid men in the White House. By 1989 I had even stopped watching for them. I had embarrassed the skulkers and their agencies by exposing them in print often enough that they no longer found it politic to follow me.

I should have been more alert that quiet afternoon in 1989

when I became a police statistic. Seven blocks from the White House, in broad daylight, within sight of scores of people, I was struck on the head with a pipe and knocked to my knees by a young man who probably wanted my money to buy crack. Unarmed people rushed to my assistance.

I was physically dazed and emotionally stunned. My notorious face was recognizable and often attracted friendly waves and calls of "Hi, Jack!" from total strangers on the street. I was accustomed to having people stop me to chat or vent their frustrations about something I had written in the newspaper. Yet here was a man, barely out of boyhood, who didn't know me and didn't care to chat about Watergate or Iran-Contra. In a fraction of a second, I understood the deep fear of the average American that he or she could at any moment become the victim of senseless, violent crime at the hands of a stranger.

Mine was a simple mugging. Every American lives a far worse nightmare. You are Herbert Clutter, and you live on a farm in Kansas. You and your family are respectable people, churchgoers, people who have done nobody harm and have no reason to expect anyone to wish you evil. And then one night two drifters, chronic losers, not bright, invade your home and kill your whole family. In cold blood.

You are Sharon Tate, or you are Rosemary LaBianca. You live well in the hills above Los Angeles. You live peacefully. You, Sharon, are pregnant. You cannot imagine that anyone hates you or has any reason to want you dead. And then one night a deluded band of drug-besotted "hippies" dispatched by a mentally deranged Charles Manson invades your home and kills everyone in the house. Helter-skelter.

You awake in the night. Some tiny noise has interrupted your sleep. You've had the nightmare many times that someone is in your bedroom. This time it's real. You choke with terror. Your heart all but stops. Finally it does stop, as the knife penetrates your chest.

And so on. Senseless killings, innocent people killed for no reason.

Then there are the innocent people killed for a reason.

You are behind the counter of your little neighborhood convenience store. A man enters. He demands nothing. He just kills you, and then takes what he wants.

You awake to feel the hand of the rapist covering your mouth. You beg him not to. He does it just the same. As you lie in tears and agony, he says good-bye to you with a 9mm slug in your face.

A young man says he admires your jacket. He wants it. You say no, it's yours. He pulls a Saturday-night special and empties it into you.

A driver runs a stop sign and nearly hits you. You lean on your horn. He jumps from his car and begins shooting. The bullets crash through your windshield and through your throat.

You are in your neighborhood pharmacy having a prescription filled. In come two kids with guns. They demand drugs from the pharmacist, kill him when he refuses, and then kill you because you are a witness.

And so on.

All these scenarios, you might like to believe, could end differently if only you had a gun. If only you could shoot first, or shoot back. If you had a gun, not only could you defend yourself, you might have the personal satisfaction of shooting down some killer with a record, some rapist, some punk with no feeling for human life . . . some *animal* that deserved to die.

Since 1871, the National Rifle Association (NRA) has been defending your right to own the gun you could use to shoot that animal. It began innocuously enough with two Civil War veterans of the Union army who incorporated the NRA "to promote rifle practice and for this purpose to provide a suitable range or ranges in the vicinity of New York." The founders persuaded the New York legislature to appropriate money to buy land for a rifle range on Long Island. At first successful, the NRA became moribund within twenty years, partly because it lost the support of the state government. In 1892 it deeded its rifle range to the state and disbanded. A little later, however, interest in target shooting increased, and the NRA was revived.

Today the NRA has 3.5 million members led by a tight cabal for whom there is no such thing as compromise. To them the Second Amendment to the Constitution is the most important right the Founding Fathers handed down to us. This right eclipses all others because of the gun's power to defend the primacy of the individual against the capriciousness of government. A nation forged in armed revolution cannot take lightly the right to keep and bear arms because one never knows when armed revolution could again be necessary.

For the NRA, the fight against tyranny never ended. Assuming the current leadership believes what it says and is not just using its anti-gun-control campaign to line its pockets, it seems to be guided by an apocalyptic vision. Here is an excerpt from an NRA "Special Report" to its membership:

THE FINAL WAR HAS BEGUN.

A DOCUMENT SECRETLY DELIVERED TO ME reveals frightening evidence that the full-scale war to **CRUSH** your gun rights has not only begun, but is well underway. . . . What's more, dozens of federal gun ban bills suggest this final assault has begun—not just to ban all handguns or all semi-automatics but to **ELIMINATE** private firearm ownership completely and forever . . .

WHAT YOU MUST DO AT ONCE:

1. BURY CONGRESS WITH YOUR LETTERS! Write and ask your congressmen to vote against these gun bans. . . .

2. DEAFEN CONGRESS WITH YOUR CALLS! Tell your congressmen about the secret anti-gun agenda to abolish gun ownership in America.

[The third thing you must do at once, according to the report, is get every gun owner you know to send money to join the NRA or to renew or upgrade **"Your Value-Packed NRA Membership."**]

Confiscate, Disarm, Destroy.

HARASSMENT, LAWSUITS, AND CRIMINAL-IZATION of lawful gun owners. While armed, violent **CRIMINALS** rage through a defenseless society, the Second Amendment goes up in flames. That's the tomorrow your children face. Only you can stop it, through NRA membership. . . .

GUN OWNERS, STAY FOCUSED
THE FIGHT FOR OUR FREEDOMS
IS FAR FROM OVER!

Even when the NRA is doing nothing more than selling insurance, the sales pitch is an apocalyptic vision of a threat to basic constitutional rights. Here's part of another letter to the membership:

> Dear NRA Member,
>
> They try to take away our right to bear arms. And we fight back. Now we're threatened with our right to use the best doctors and hospitals. THE NRA THINKS IT'S TIME TO FIGHT AGAIN.
> And we've armed ourselves with the best, lowest-cost cancer care protection we could find. For as little as $3.67 a month.

Apocalyptic and a bargain to boot. The NRA leadership consistently writes down to its membership:

> The gun banners simply don't like you. They don't trust you. They don't want you to own a gun. And they'll stop at nothing until they've forced you to turn over your guns to the government. . . . <u>if the NRA fails to restore our Second Amendment freedoms, the attacks will begin on freedom of religion, freedom of speech, freedom from unreasonable search and seizure</u>. . . . **Congress must be forced to restore the Constitution, repeal the gun bans, investigate abuses by government agents and focus the public debate on criminal control, not gun control. . . . Or what we're seeing now will only be a momentary patch of sunshine on the road to doom for the Second Amendment and our Constitution.**

An excerpt from another NRA fund-raising letter reads:

"The time has come for the showdown of the century. Will you fight or will you fold?"

Exactly what impact does the NRA suppose that this kind of language—with which its members are constantly bombarded—will have?

"The Final War Has Begun." What war? Rational people see no war, begun or impending. Congress must be *forced* to *restore* the Constitution? What rational person thinks the Constitution needs restoring? And by what means does the NRA expect to *force* Congress? Are the rest of us just hopelessly deluded Pollyannas, or is the NRA armed and dangerous, hell-bent on a track of paranoia?

Let's start with a basic premise. I believe that members of the NRA generally are good and intelligent people, with genuine concerns, who want to protect their rights to own guns but are willing to accept limited and reasonable restraints in the interest of public safety.

Unhappily, however, the current leadership of the NRA has changed a fellowship of sportsmen, target shooters, and hunters into an intransigent right-wing political organization that is not representative of its membership and serves them ill. What is worse, its fanatical propaganda serves the nation ill. Worse still, its unholy alliance with many members of Congress taints the legislative process. It is inconceivable that many members of the NRA know what the organization is doing and still support it—either that or the NRA has assembled as its membership 3.5 million fanatic-fringe extremists who are wholly out of touch with reality.

I don't think the latter is true. I believe the general membership of the NRA simply needs to be informed of what the organization is doing. That is my chief reason for writing this book.

Former president George Bush resigned his membership in the NRA in May 1995 after its executive vice president, Wayne LaPierre, distributed a letter calling agents of the Bureau of Alcohol, Tobacco and Firearms "jack-booted thugs." The former president was not alone in his contempt for LaPierre's rabid rhetoric. Colorado Senator Ben Nighthorse Campbell, elected as a Democrat but now a Republican, also resigned his NRA membership, as did General Norman Schwarzkopf. Michigan Congressman John D. Dingell, a longtime opponent of gun control, resigned his seat on the NRA board of directors.

Senator Campbell said of the NRA, "They've become abusive, accusatory, sick, violent, threatening bullies. They want absolute subservience, and they're not going to get it from me."

General Schwarzkopf said, "[The NRA has become] very inflexible and almost radical; they appeal to a fringe element of gun owners."

I am not an anti-gun fanatic. Far from it. In the West, where I grew up, guns were a part of life, and guns were to be found in nearly every home. I have owned and used guns all my life. I taught my children to shoot. I am one of that great majority of Americans who would firmly oppose any attempt to take away the guns that law-abiding men and women legitimately own.

I am well aware, however, that the myth of the American West—that of fast-draw artists and rugged individualists who went about armed to the teeth—is exactly what I've just called it: a myth. Only a minority of Western men carried six-shooters, and only a tiny minority of them could hit anything. The truth is that guns and ammunition were too expensive for most frontier people. The majority of ranchers and farmers didn't even own a handgun, much less shoot off expensive ammunition during the target practice they would have had to do to become fast and accurate.

I share the concern of the American people that violence has become endemic in our country. The first duty of government is to protect its people against violent crime, and right now the government cannot do it. It is simply true that the police cannot be everywhere all the time. What happens between the time you call 911 and the moment when even the most efficient police force is there to help? Is the answer that every American should be armed? I don't think so.

On that afternoon in Washington, if I'd had a .44 caliber Magnum automatic in a shoulder holster, it would have done me no good. I was down. My attacker had fled as people who had seen the incident rushed to my assistance. It might be a satisfying scenario to imagine myself dropping that urban animal with a well-placed shot, but it's a fantasy. I would just as likely have hit some innocent person on the street—more likely, in fact, because there were more of them.

I empathize, on the one hand, with Americans who do not want to give up their guns for one reason or another. I join them in opposition to laws that would compel us to surrender them. Many of my friends keep handguns in their nightstands. Others have them in their desks. Although statistics clearly indicate that they or their family members are more likely to harm themselves than they are to fend off a criminal with a handgun, still, that is a decision people are entitled to make.

On the other hand, I favor reasonable limitations on the right to own and carry guns in order to prevent gun accidents and, as far as possible, to prevent crime. One study, done some years ago, shows that one-third of all new handguns manufactured in the United States are used at least once in committing a violent crime during their useful lives. In 1992 alone, 930,700 handgun crimes were committed, 13,200 of which were homicides.

Polls show that at least 75 percent of the American people—some polls show as many as 95 percent—favor limited, reasonable gun control, though LaPierre describes all such polls as "phony." For the most part, they don't get these controls. Why? Because the NRA almost always wins its fights against gun control, which it does by constant mass mailings and by vicious vilification of anyone who gets on its list of enemies.

Although I entertain some doubt that instigating waiting periods and conducting criminal background checks before issuing a gun will make America a safe place to be, I see in those measures no unreasonable impediment to a citizen's right to keep and bear arms.

Similarly, I see no reason why citizens need to keep and bear assault rifles. The term *assault rifle* is admittedly difficult to define, but some weapons simply have no purpose but to kill people, and no hunter or target shooter is harmed by a ban on them.

I see no reason why anyone needs bullets capable of penetrating the Kevlar vests worn by many police officers—the so-called cop-killer bullets.

I see no reason why every attempt to impose a reasonable, even an innocuous, limitation on gun purchases should be screamed about as an apocalyptic event—a step on the road to banning all firearms in America.

I see no reason why the current leadership of the NRA is blind to the difference between reasonable limitations on gun ownership and "the disarming of America."

I see no reason why the current leadership of the NRA should obsessively trumpet the totally discredited notion that the Second Amendment to the Constitution of the United States affords citizens a right to keep and bear arms, subject to no reasonable limitation that may be written into law. Beginning in the last century, the courts have repeatedly rejected such an interpretation of the Second Amendment and no respected authority on constitutional law accepts this wild idea.

I see no reason why the current leadership of the NRA should launch intemperate attacks on members of Congress who do not hew 100 percent to their line. Why, for example, should they call Representative Charles Schumer "the criminal's Congressman?"

I see no reason why the executive vice president of the NRA should call agents of the Bureau of Alcohol, Tobacco and Firearms "jack-booted thugs," or how he could, in that same letter, justify saying, "In Clinton's administration, if you have a badge, you have the government's go-ahead to harass, intimidate, even murder law-abiding citizens." [Emphasis his]

Are these opinions shared by the general membership of the National Rifle Association? I don't think so. In my experience, members of the NRA are responsible citizens and are as shocked as I am by the extremist rhetoric of its current leaders. They don't want laws that would take away their guns, but they know perfectly well that Congress is not going to pass any such law and that the president—including *this* president, Bill Clinton—would veto the law if it were passed.

Most NRA members must not know who has taken over their organization, and for what purpose. This book is dedicated to them, in the hope they will use the information it contains to reclaim the National Rifle Association for the honest, respectable, and concerned men and women who are at its core.

CHAPTER TWO

ELBOWING THE WAY
TO PROMINENCE

How did the NRA get from those two old Union soldiers to the powerful congressional arm-twister it is today? The same way any self-respecting lobby group rises to the top in Washington—by padding its constituency with millions of members who pay cheap dues and remain largely uninformed and uninvolved while a loud-mouthed staff in Washington pushes its own agenda and protects its ample budget.

The NRA's first entry into lobbying came in 1911, when it opposed the enactment of New York's Sullivan Law, which prohibited handgun ownership by anyone who did not have a permit. The NRA used an argument that would become its first article of faith: Guns don't kill people, people kill people. In fact, NRA officers argued soberly that the automobile, not the gun, was responsible for the great increase in crime that accompanied Prohibition.

Later, the position taken by the NRA in the National Firearms Act of 1934 would send its present leadership into apoplexy. The NRA's then-executive vice president, Milton Reckord, told the

House Ways and Means Committee, "We believe that the machine gun, submachine gun, sawed-off shotgun, and dangerous and deadly weapons could all be included in any kind of bill, and no matter how drastic, we will support it. The association I represent is absolutely favorable to reasonable legislation."

Even so, the NRA managed to strip handgun restrictions from the bill through a mail-and-telegram campaign of the kind it constantly uses today.

After World War II the NRA greatly expanded its membership by appealing to hunters to join. Traditionally, it had been an organization of target shooters; now it invited hunters into the fold and instituted a hunter safety-training program.

In 1963 Lee Harvey Oswald bought by mail order the rifle he allegedly used to assassinate President John F. Kennedy. Twice, Connecticut Senator Thomas Dodd attempted to secure the passage of legislation to limit the sale of weapons. The NRA warned its members that the Congress was considering "anti-gun laws" that threatened the rights of "loyal Americans."

During the Cold War years, the NRA used an anti-Communist theme effectively. It argued relentlessly that the Communists wanted American civilians disarmed to facilitate a takeover of the United States.

The murders of Dr. Martin Luther King, Jr., and Senator Robert Kennedy increased the public outcry for more gun control. Although legislation was passed banning the importation of certain guns, nothing was done about domestically manufactured weapons. Even a bill to ban Saturday-night specials—cheap, shoddily manufactured, and unsafe handguns—failed in Congress in 1972.

The NRA actually endorsed the ban on Saturday-night specials. It was the last time the organization would endorse any form of gun control. In 1977 the NRA was taken over by a faction of angry Second Amendment fundamentalists. Suddenly the nature of the organization changed radically. What had been essentially an association of gun enthusiasts and sportsmen became an ugly, fanatic band, far to the right of right.

The new voice of the NRA would be that of Harlon Carter. At the organization's 1977 convention, held in Cincinnati, Carter successfully led an insurgent group of members in a complete takeover of the NRA.

To head the NRA's Institute for Legislative Action, its lobbying arm, Carter appointed his friend Neal Knox, who was even more iron-willed and uncompromising than Carter himself. Knox was, in fact, so intransigent that he made too many enemies on Capitol Hill, and the NRA was eventually forced to fire him. It was a temporary setback for Knox. He was returned to the board of directors in 1991, where he continues to influence NRA policy.

Besides making the NRA an ideological organization, Carter made it a thriving business by selling a wide variety of merchandise, including hats, caps, belt buckles, key chains, coffee mugs, and, especially, insurance.

It was Carter and Knox's intention to increase membership to such numbers that politicians would be afraid to ignore the NRA. In this they very largely succeeded. Membership now exceeds three million, even after losing perhaps 300,000 members as a result of the "jack-booted thugs" letter.

Only a minority of NRA members, though, actually buy its

ideology. The majority of members are interested in articles and stories about guns and hunting, so they look forward to their issues of *The American Rifleman* or *American Hunter,* which they receive as part of their membership. Like any hobbyists, they study the ads run in these magazines and wonder if they can afford one more deer rifle or a handsome new pump-action shotgun.

Evidence of how little interest members really take in the affairs of the NRA can be found in its election returns. The balloting is conducted by mail. In 1995 the top vote-getter won her seat on the board by polling 69,767 votes, according to the numbers published in the August 1995 issue of *American Hunter.* Add to that the number of votes—43,741—polled by the biggest loser in the election and you get an idea of how many members voted. About 3.8 percent of the NRA membership cared enough about its leadership and policies to mail in a ballot.

The NRA says 24,000 members attended its annual convention, gun show, and gala held in 1995 in Phoenix. That constitutes .8 percent of its membership. Eight-tenths of one percent. But that eight-tenths of one percent were angry. Some of them shouted the slogan that NRA means "Not Ready to Apologize." They were believers, too. Many of them were vocal in insisting the language the NRA uses is fully justified. Even when the leadership tried to tone down its rhetoric a bit, the conventioneers did not tone down theirs.

If a greater percentage of the majority of NRA members would make their voices heard, however, the organization would moderate its stand and cooperate with efforts to enact reasonable limitations on gun ownership and use while continuing to take a firm stand against laws that would unreasonably interfere with the right of Americans to own firearms.

The present leadership of the NRA is driven by three people: Wayne LaPierre, Neal Knox, and Tanya Metaksa.

Harlon Carter established the executive vice presidency of the NRA as its most conspicuous and powerful office. That was the office he held. After his retirement, there was a period of infighting in the NRA. My sources tell me that the infighting continues today; the organization is not nearly as monolithic as it appears from the outside. Despite internal squabbles, LaPierre has held on to the office of executive vice president since 1991.

LaPierre, age forty-five, is paid $190,000 a year. This man, who wrote the "jack-booted thugs" letter and is the author of other rhetoric no less fiery or conciliatory is not a fire-breathing ogre. People who know him and people who have interviewed him describe him as mild-mannered. He speaks convincingly and calmly. Neal Knox, who comes closer to being a fire-breathing ogre, says that sometimes LaPierre is "too nice." LaPierre is divorced and has no children; he says he regrets that his work all but denies him a personal life. Indeed, he has suggested that he is not going to remain at his job for the rest of his active life. He loves ice cream and says, apparently not altogether facetiously, that he would like to retire and buy an ice cream shop.

Neal Knox, board member and second vice president, is a believer. He was Harlon Carter's disciple but broke with Carter—or rather, Carter broke with him—because Carter was not hard-line enough for Knox. A late-middle-aged man who wears conservative, three-piece suits and wire-frame glasses, Knox is a hero to the NRA's hardest liners. He might have

LaPierre's job except for a serious deficiency in his makeup—he has no political instincts. He is rigidly unwilling to compromise on the slightest thing, and he thinks he can browbeat congressmen who do not accept his every dictate.

In the December 1994 issue of *Shotgun News,* Knox published a column suggesting that the murders of President John F. Kennedy, Senator Robert Kennedy, and Martin Luther King, Jr., could have been elements of an anti-gun conspiracy.

"Is it possible," he wrote, "that some of these incidents could have been created for the purpose of disarming the people of the free world? With drugs and evil intent, it's possible. Rampant paranoia on my part? Maybe. But there have been far too many coincidences to ignore."

The current head of the NRA's Institute for Legislative Action (ILA) is Tanya Metaksa, fifty-eight, another rigid hard-liner known for being aggressive and uncompromising to the point of rudeness. She is a lifelong activist, a volunteer for Barry Goldwater in 1964, and later a leader in the Connecticut gun lobby. She has profited from her activism. Her ILA salary is estimated at $150,000.

Metaksa wants no one to diminish her commitment to the cause. When her unusual name is often misspelled or mispronounced, she offers a way to remember the last four letters: "It's AK, like in AK-47, and SA, like in semiautomatic."

Metaksa was put on the defensive in 1995 when it was disclosed that her Internet bulletin board, called Bullet 'N Board, carried a set of detailed instructions for building a deadly bomb from a baby-food jar packed with readily obtainable materials.

The recipe was offered by an Internet contributor who called himself or herself Warmaster. I quote a part of it—not the specific ingredients, though. Too many people already know what those are:

> These simple, powerful bombs are not very well known even though all the materials can be easily obtained (even by minors). These things are so [expletive] powerful that they can destroy a car. The explosion can actually twist and mangle the frame. They are extremely deadly and can very easily kill you and blow the side of . . . the house out if you mess up while building it. . . . For antipersonnel, tape nails to the side of the thing. . . . If the explosion doesn't get 'em then the glass will. If the glass don't get 'em then the nails will. . . . If you want to spread some chaos, this little bomb is the way to go.

After several months of flak over carrying the recipe, Metaksa quietly killed Bullet 'N Board. Neal Knox suggested that the *Washington Post* may have planted the recipe to embarrass the NRA.

Incidentally, I am highly skeptical of Warmaster's bomb. People with experience tell me it is extremely unlikely the bomb would do what he or she says. What is more likely, as Warmaster emphatically warns, is that a person trying to build it would blow his hands off.

In any case, it was hardly responsible citizenship for Tanya Metaksa to have left the bomb recipe on Bullet 'N Board for even one day after she learned it was on there. Those in Congress who profess to worry about pornography on the Internet should be more alarmed over instructions on how to build a bomb.

Sometimes the positions taken by the NRA are outside all imagining. In 1991 Sears offered a line of stuffed animals as Christmas toys for children. A deal was cut for 8 percent of the wholesale purchase price of the stuffed animals to be donated to the Humane Society of the United States. The NRA and other lobbying groups criticized Sears for being "insensitive" to hunters. Under pressure, Sears caved in and withdrew the stuffed animals. The Humane Society protested the NRA's "macho bullying," but the toys remained off the market.

Such positions require much self-delusion and not a little bit of tinkering with the truth. Nothing more than a hasty reading of NRA rhetoric demonstrates that. To fudge the facts successfully, however, you must be skillful. One NRA tactic is so inept as to be comic.

For years, one "Theodore H. Fiddleman" has sent letters to publications from the *Washington Post* to the *New York Times*. Fiddleman has been eloquent in his vitriolic attacks on President Clinton and on the Bureau of Alcohol, Tobacco and Firearms, among others. For example, he accused federal agents of a tendency to "confuse executing warrants and executing women and children."

There is no such person as Theodore H. Fiddleman. It is a pseudonym used by Paul H. Blackman, an employee of Tanya Metaksa's and the ILA. At first, Blackman denied he was Fiddleman but eventually admitted it. Why the pen name? Because it was easy to get letters to the editor and guest editorials published if the editors were unaware of his NRA affiliation. He added that NRA employees were under pressure to get such pieces published. Tanya Metaksa emphatically denied she knew anything about it, but a former employee of the NRA said such ghost-writing was common and was no secret within the organization.

This scam allowed the NRA to publicize its ideas without having to take responsibility for them. "Fiddleman" could make any outrageous charges the NRA wanted and no one at the NRA could be questioned about his "facts," nor would any of the mainstream NRA membership be alarmed by what they read.

When an organization has to duck responsibility for its own points of view, that is an indicator that all is not well with the organization. This is true of the NRA.

For one thing, it is running out of allies. The principal police organizations have condemned its hysterical rhetoric and have distanced themselves from it. Prominent members have resigned.

In May, President Clinton called on the NRA to donate the money it received from its "jack-booted thugs" fund-raising letter to the families of slain police officers. The NRA scorned the idea. Right-wing presidential wanna-be Pat Buchanan didn't. Campaigning in Texas, Buchanan said, "I have no problem with that idea." He also said, "I would not agree with any disparaging attacks on federal agents."

My research has led me to believe that the NRA has a much bigger problem than its dwindling ranks of support among the movers and shakers in Washington. Its accounting books are none too healthy. The NRA has increased its membership hugely since 1991, and its ILA has become the nation's largest political action committee (PAC). During the same period, however, it has depleted the cash reserve it had in 1991 and has accumulated a cash deficit of either $55.3 million or $71.9 million, depending on which set of accounting numbers you choose to believe.

In 1992 the NRA reported a deficit of $34 million. In 1993 it reported a deficit of $32.7 million.

In 1990 the NRA had a nest egg of more than $92 million invested in blue-chip stocks and bonds. It sold off much of that nest egg to cover its budget gap until the nest egg was only $41 million. How can an organization that has investment assets of $41 million be in trouble? Simple. All but $3 million of those assets are pledged as loan collateral.

The situation may be worse than that. On July 9, 1995, the *New York Times* published a letter from NRA life member David Ross, a former member of the U.S. Olympic shooting team. Here is part of his letter:

> The large $92 million "nest egg" referred to is not a surplus in any case. This "nest egg" did not arise from the accumulation of profits but largely from selling life memberships, which require an up-front cash payment. . . . In return, lifetime benefits in the N.R.A. (including a magazine subscription) are provided to this class of membership.
>
> The N.R.A. has sold many such life memberships and, since it collects far more than it costs to provide services to life members, the excess appears among the association's assets as "investments" (marketable securities). This "nest egg" is being held to provide funds for future services due these life members.
>
> The N.R.A. has spent or borrowed against this fund and therefore has little or no reserve left to provide the promised future services to members, which the N.R.A. has been doing for some time.
>
> Among the most obvious efforts to cut costs has

been withdrawal as the national governing body for shooting (in connection with a controversy with the U.S. Olympic Committee over staffing and funding) and the reduction of the publication of the N.R.A. magazines from monthly to bimonthly.

The management of the N.R.A., to sustain the level of legislative activity, has adopted a strategy of spending itself nearly into bankruptcy. At some point soon funds will not be available to continue to provide services promised to life members.

There is, in fact, a good deal of confusion within the NRA about what assets it has and how much it spends. By no means am I suggesting that someone is stealing money, only that the NRA's bookkeeping appears to be extremely sloppy.

In its 1992 financial report to members, the NRA listed "total operating expenditures" at $141.5 million. The treasurer's report to the board of directors, however, reported "actual costs of operation" as $86.1 million. The association reported a third figure to the Internal Revenue Service (IRS): $139 million.

The NRA continues to spend more each year than it receives in income.

Where does all this money go? Essentially it goes to two places: buying influence in Washington and recruiting new members.

Until annual dues were recently raised to $35, they were $25. Yet according to reports filed with the IRS, membership promotional costs are $97 per new member. Presumably the difference will be recouped when the member goes on paying dues year after year. Not so. In a report to its board of directors in 1994, the membership committee of the NRA admitted that only 43 percent of new members renewed their memberships for a second year.

The National Rifle Association's high-powered lobbying does not come cheap. Our members of Congress cannot be bought for a pittance. The ILA conducts its own fund drives to help raise money, but at the end of 1994 its cumulative budget shortfall was $38.7 million—roughly 70 percent of the NRA's overall deficit.

Concerned members of the NRA came forward with copies of certain documents, including a letter written by Max W. Goodwin, chairman of the financial committee, to Thomas Washington, president, which read: "The disintegration of the assets of the N.R.A. under current spending policies have eroded our future viability [and are] a cause for great concern. The management, the board of directors and the National Rifle Association itself all may fail."

In July 1995, Dun & Bradstreet, the nation's leading credit-rating agency, gave the NRA a rating of 9, the lowest possible rating—one reserved for companies having extreme financial difficulties. In the report Dun & Bradstreet noted that the NRA paid its creditors fifteen days late on average. The report concluded, "This business has a deficit tangible net worth."

"What that means," said James Nesbitt, an accountant with BDO Seidman who specializes in auditing nonprofit groups, "is that Dun & Bradstreet sees an organization that has dug itself into a deep hole." It also means the NRA will find it more difficult to do business with banks and contractors.

Wayne LaPierre insisted the organization is stronger than ever, and Tanya Metaksa said the NRA is in "great shape." Even so, only a month before the Dun & Bradstreet report came out, LaPierre had sent a letter to its members saying, "[the] NRA needs to put $812,000 in the bank within 30 days." He warned of huge program cuts if the NRA did not get the money.

I don't know whether the $812,000 came in. The NRA is secretive about how much money its various fund-raising activities generate. For example, it has refused to say how much money the "jack-booted thugs" letter raised.

The truth is that the NRA is quite informal about the way it handles money. Some former members of its board of directors claim that staff and board members have used their NRA affiliation for personal profit.

In 1993 the NRA paid $194,000 on a no-bid consulting contract to a company called Bullet Communications. The majority stockholder and president of Bullet Communications was Tanya Metaksa, who at the time was a member of the board of directors of the NRA. Then she resigned from the board and became executive director of the NRA's Institute for Legislative Action. In 1994, while she was drawing her salary from the NRA, the NRA paid her company another $90,000.

From 1991 to 1994, while serving as a member of the NRA board of directors, Neal Knox solicited contributions from NRA members, promising to be their "personal lobbyist." These contributions were to be paid directly to him, not to the NRA. Knox protested, "I don't see how in the world that can be construed as making money off being a board member."

In 1993 the NRA gave $100,000 to an affiliated organization called Unified Sportsmen of Florida. Marion Hammer, a member of the NRA board, was executive director of Unified Sportsmen.

That same year Unified Sportsmen made a personal loan of $30,000 to Hammer at an interest rate of 3 percent. The purpose of the loan was to help her to buy a home.

At least two other board members have taken fees or received money for running NRA ads in their magazines.

Wayne LaPierre's book, *Guns, Crime and Freedom,* was promoted by an NRA postcard mailing. If the NRA paid 29 cents postage and sent the mailing to all members, the cost of simply sending it out had to exceed three-quarters of a million dollars. Add to that the fees for printing and related services, and the cost of this promotion may have approached $1 million. It is highly doubtful the book earned that much in sales. Even if LaPierre gives all his royalties to the NRA, it is extremely unlikely the organization will recover even a fraction of the cost of that mailing.

LaPierre has not responded to requests from me to be interviewed on this or any other subject.

It may be possible that none of this is illegal. But it is highly questionable back-scratching, and the NRA membership should know about these deals. It is no wonder the NRA constantly bombards its members with panicked appeals for more money.

On April 5, 1995, Tanya Metaksa signed a fund-raising letter saying she had "devastating news" about a "financial crisis" that could "spell disaster." In a postscript to her letter she wrote, "We would appreciate your keeping the contents of the NRA-ILA first quarter financial report to yourself. We don't want the anti-gun forces to get wind of this financial crisis."

That is what the "jack-booted thugs" letter was also—a near-hysterical appeal for money. In it, LaPierre wrote:

The truth is, NRA members have been hardened by legislative battles. And only NRA members have the courage, the conviction to draw the line in the sand.

That's why I'm hoping you can take a few moments to sign and date the enclosed Petitions and return them to me with your special contribution of $15, $20, $25, $35, $50 or more in the enclosed postage-paid envelope today. Or you can charge by phone . . .

Please tell me you're ready to take the next step by returning your signed Petitions to Congress and special gift to me in the enclosed postage-paid envelope . . .

P.S. As a special thank you for making a special contribution of $25 or more, I'd like to send you a copy of my national best-selling book, *Guns, Crime and Freedom* . . .

His "best-selling book" was promoted by the NRA mail campaign I described above. The postcards were enclosed in an "urgent message"—all NRA messages are "urgent"—to the membership. Charging that the mass media would not review the LaPierre book, the NRA asked its members to send their newspapers preprinted postcards demanding that they publish reviews of *Guns, Crime and Freedom*. This was part of a "major assault on the media beachhead." The newspapers generally resented the pressure and ignored the book. That the newspaper editors dug in their heels was unfortunate. The book deserved to be objectively considered by the critics, and the NRA should not have had to resort to its own marketing to get the word out. The critics also stubbornly ignored the counterweight to LaPierre's book, *NRA: Money, Firepower and Fear*, by Josh Sugarman, executive director of the Violence Policy Center, with whose permission I have drawn on that book for some of the history of the NRA.

In the summer of 1995, in fulfillment of the NRA's fear that Big Brother is everywhere, the IRS began a full audit of the organization. It is registered as a nonprofit organization that raises money through membership dues and donations. Dues and contributions paid to the NRA are not tax deductible. An affiliate, the NRA Foundation, is registered as a charitable organization with education as its purpose. Gifts to the Foundation are deductible. It is generally unlawful for a charitable organization to distribute funds to a noncharitable affiliate. If it does, it must track the funds to be sure the noncharitable affiliate used them for charitable purposes. This is what the IRS wants to know. Does money taken in for a charitable purpose wind up paying the cost of lobbying?

Whenever a nonprofit organization and a charity commingle their funds, careful accounting must be done to ascertain how the money is used. The problem is especially acute when the same people constitute the leadership for both organizations, as is the case with the NRA and the NRA Foundation.

The Foundation does transfer millions of dollars annually to the NRA. Most of the money is used for NRA educational programs, such as teaching women self-defense and teaching children gun safety, an NRA spokesman says. If it is true, that is lawful and proper.

The IRS will look at other problems, some of them arising from the fact that the NRA has filed returns that are not complete. There is also a question of how advertising revenues have been used and reported.

The NRA has many sources of money besides dues. For example, a recent eighty-four page issue of *American Rifleman* carried thirty-five pages of advertising—this in addition to the inside front cover and both the inside and outside of the back cover. The NRA lends its membership list and logo to insurance companies and a credit-card issuer, for which of course it receives substantial fees. It also sells an extensive line of merchandise, including caps, shirts, jackets, vests, tie clips, belt buckles, coffee mugs, pocketknives, books, and videos. Members should be asking where all that money goes.

In the face of the IRS audit, Max Goodwin, chairman of the NRA finance committee; Michael McCabe, NRA general counsel for the past fifteen years; and Bob Clarke, former chief of staff, resigned from the NRA. Warren Johnson, formerly a member of the NRA board of directors, said, "There are leaders who see this organization going down the tubes. There is a lot of fear about what the IRS is going to find."

Neal Knox says the audit is just another tactic the Clinton administration is using to attack a patriotic organization. This overlooks the fact that the IRS is also currently investigating the American Association of Retired Persons and the Sierra Club on largely the same grounds.

Tanya Metaksa, whose frantic appeal for contributions is quoted on page 36, shrugs off the audit and the deficit, saying the NRA has no financial problems.

Wayne LaPierre denounced reports of financial problems at the NRA. "We're healthy, strong, and growing," he said.

I have contacted the NRA repeatedly, citing my documentation of its financial difficulties and offering the NRA an opportunity to show me proof that it is thriving. I promised the NRA that if it would show me documentation demonstrating that the suggestions of financial problems are false, I would publish that documentation. As I write, the NRA has not responded.

Always there has been a faction of NRA activists who abhor the ideological bond it has become and want to return it to an association of hobbyists and sportsmen. They have never given up, though they have repeatedly been defeated by the ideologues.

What do the members want? The fact that 43 percent of the new members recruited in 1993 did not renew for a second year is suggestive. The extremely low turnout for NRA elections is even more suggestive. It is entirely possible that the membership, if it took the trouble to make itself heard, could make a world of difference.

In the meantime, though, the NRA has maintained a remarkable record of keeping its secrets.

For example, Jeff Cooper has been a member of the board of directors since 1984. He was nominated by the NRA nominating committee, so he has the association's endorsement. In fact, *American Rifleman* published an article saying what a great man he is. He writes a newsletter called *Jeff Cooper's Commentaries* and a monthly column for *Guns & Ammo* magazine. The text is available on the NRA's Internet bulletin board, GUN-TALK. Here are some quotations from the writings of Jeff Cooper:

> . . . the radical rise in the murder rate in the L.A. basin should be viewed with due reference to the Good Riddance factor. . . . A certain amount of subjective guesswork is involved, of course, but the consensus is that no more than five to ten people in a hundred who die by gunfire in Los Angeles are any loss to society. . . . Pearl Harbor Day slipped by without much notice. . . .

Apparently the Nips are playing it smart by entreating us to give up our guns. They could not defeat us in battle, so they are now doing their best to destroy us politically by abrogating our constitution. They cannot accomplish this by themselves, but they are getting a lot of help from our wimp culture. . . . Los Angeles and Ho Chi Min [sic] City have declared themselves sister cities. It makes sense—they are both Third World metropolises formerly occupied by Americans.

Perhaps the most distressing aspect of the NRA is the unholy alliances it has formed.One of those is perhaps not entirely the NRA's fault. Any organization that recruits heavily is apt to attract its share of kooks. Unhappily, its rhetoric attracts those kooks from the militia movement in particular and from racist and anti-Semitic groups as well. Because the NRA proclaims itself the guardian of "good" Americans' "right" to own guns, it appeals to those who believe they must arm themselves against whatever. Because these people join the NRA and are activists within it, the NRA is tainted.

It could try to clean its house. Instead, it proclaims "The Final War Has Begun. Now They've Got Your Number. Confiscate, Disarm, Destroy." Instead of trying to keep hate fanatics out, the NRA consciously appeals to them.

The other unholy alliance is with the right wing of the Republican Party. Would-be candidates for the Republican nomination for president of the United States know they cannot win the nomination in the face of opposition from (1) the so-called pro-life movement, (2) the Christian right, and (3) the anti-gun-control hard-liners.

When it was suggested to Newt Gingrich that he should help pass some moderate gun-control legislation, he laughed and reminded the person making the suggestion that the anti-gun-control people were a part of his coalition. He wrote a "Dear Tanya" letter to Tanya Metaksa, promising her that no gun-control legislation would ever reach the floor of the House while he is Speaker. "Let me say that this is both a discussion among friends but more importantly among like-minded individuals."

The candidate for the Republican nomination who has most closely associated himself with the NRA is Senator Phil Gramm. He is something of an NRA icon. The cover of the March 1995 issue of *American Rifleman* featured a color photograph of him in the company of Wayne LaPierre and Tanya Metaksa. Displayed across the lower part of the picture in large letters were the words *freedom fighters*. Senator Gramm has received more than $442,000 in campaign contributions from the NRA since 1979. (Senator Bob Dole has received $58,000.)

The NRA takes credit for the election of the Republican Congress. Since it contributed $1,442,519 to select Republican candidates, it undoubtedly did have an influence.

Another example of NRA intransigence is its treatment of Texas congressman Jack Brooks. For years Brooks had been an NRA hero, a staunch opponent of gun control. In 1992 the NRA Political Victory Fund contributed $9,900 to his campaign—typically, though not always, its maximum gift to a campaign. Then Congressman Brooks voted for the 1994 crime bill, which was written to ban an additional nineteen assault weapons. In the 1994 election, the NRA Political Victory Fund gave Brooks $4,950 and his opponent, Steve Stockman, $9,900. The

NRA really does ask, "What have you done for me *lately*?"

Over the years the NRA has expanded its agenda. For decades it was a one-issue lobby opposed to any form of gun control. Now it spends millions of dollars to elect right-wing Republicans. In the 1994 congressional campaign, it abandoned Democrats and moderate Republicans who had for years opposed gun control. Besides Jack Brooks, former Speaker of the House Tom Foley was opposed by the NRA, even though he had been a consistent supporter of its anti-gun-control position. And these are only two examples. The NRA Political Victory Fund spent more money in 1994 than any other PAC, and for right-wing Republicans almost without exception.

When the new Congress assembled, NRA lobbyists declared "payback" time and arrogantly descended on Congress, aggressively flexing their muscles. The chief items on the NRA agenda were immediate repeal of the Brady Law waiting period for gun purchases and the assault-weapons ban. On these items there was to be no compromise. The NRA demanded these repeals and was confident it would get them.

This in spite of the opposition of virtually every law enforcement group in the country. "It's a matter of survival for police officers," said an officer of the International Association of Police Chiefs. The repeal is opposed as well by the National Association of Counties, the National League of Cities, and the U.S. Conference of Mayors.

Tanya Metaksa mocked the police chiefs. "The rank-and-file officers support us," she insisted, implying that rank-and-file cops don't want a waiting period before hotheads can buy guns, nor that they care whether assault weapons are on the streets.

This in spite of the fact that an NBC poll showed 76 percent of Americans opposed repealing the assault-weapons ban, with only 19 percent favoring its repeal. This in spite of the fact that a poll of gun owners in Pennsylvania found that 82 percent of them opposed repeal of a state law requiring a forty-eight-hour wait before buying a handgun. In fact, 79 percent of NRA members polled opposed repeal.

Again, Wayne LaPierre describes such polls as "phony."

The NRA seemed to be riding high until the Oklahoma City bombing sickened the vast majority of Americans and generated a revulsion against violence in general and gun violence in particular. After that, the Republican leadership quietly shelved the repeal bills.

Perhaps these leaders had taken time to study the exit polls from the 1994 election, which showed that 48 percent of the voters came from households that owned guns but that gun issues had little or no influence on their votes. Like other voters, they were concerned about the economy, health care, crime in the streets, and so forth.

There can be no doubt, however, that the NRA will demand that these gun bills be revived, if not in the current Congress then in the next. "We're not changing any tactics," said Tanya Metaksa. "We're going to have a great 1995 and an even greater 1996."

There is a dramatic irony in all this, as was noted in an editorial in the *Sacramento Bee:*

> Republicans who once ritualistically attacked Democrats for favoring "criminals' rights" now endorse policies that make life easier for violent criminals and harder for local police and their federal counterparts.

Not only are GOP leaders soon to renew their push for repeal of the assault-weapons ban, but they have vowed to roll back the Clinton plan to underwrite 100,000 new local police officers. . . .

The GOP that once accused the Democrats of being soft on crime because they embrace an anti-establishment counterculture is now soft on crime itself because it's coddling a new, gun-crazy counterculture of its own.

To comments like these, Tanya Metaksa replies that the NRA is a target of "hatred and scapegoating."

What exactly are assault weapons? The Violent Crime Control and Law Enforcement Act of 1994 defines them as follows:

As to a rifle, it must be semiautomatic, must be able to accept a detachable magazine, and must have at least two of the following five features: folding stock, pistol grip, bayonet mount, barrel threaded for flash suppressor, grenade launcher.

As to a pistol, it must be semiautomatic and able to accept a detachable magazine, and must have at least two of the following five features: magazine attaches outside of the pistol grip, barrel threaded for silencer, barrel shroud, unloaded weight of at least 50 ounces or more, semiautomatic version of a machine gun.

The definition specifically excludes any gun that is manually operated by bolt, pump, lever, or slide action and any semiautomatic rifle that cannot accept a magazine that holds more than five rounds of ammunition.

Why would anybody want or need an assault weapon? you may ask. Why, indeed?

This is the ban the NRA is pledged to repeal. This is the bill about which Senator Bob Dole wrote to Tanya Metaksa, "Repealing the ill-conceived gun ban passed as part of President Clinton's crime bill last year is one of my legislative priorities."

There can be no doubt that the NRA will be flexing its muscles again in the 1996 elections. It should take heed, however, of a poll that says 42 percent of Americans would be less likely to vote for a candidate endorsed by the NRA.

CHAPTER THREE

THE NRA'S TRUE CONSTITUTIONAL RIGHTS

You won't hear this from the National Rifle Association, but nothing in the Constitution of the United States guarantees a citizen the absolute right to bear arms. I had that reinforced for me firsthand in 1989. Back then we were naive enough to think that the worst terrorist threat against the United States would come from outsiders, possibly Middle Eastern radicals schooled in high-tech terror. (This was, of course, before the Oklahoma City bombing in 1995, which taught us that terror can be low-tech and that not all terrorists are bred outside our borders.)

In 1989 I was worried about foreign terrorists; experts had told me that our wide-open buildings and the complacent rent-a-cops who guarded them were ripe for the picking. My sources claimed it would be a piece of cake for anyone, even me, to spirit a gun into the Capitol, for instance, and pick off a U.S. senator.

Metal detectors would be no hindrance because the gun would be plastic—not a child's toy, but a sophisticated Glock pistol with a few metal parts that could be easily removed and disguised. I decided to test the theory, but I had to break the law to do so. Despite the lofty promise of the Second Amendment that I have the right to keep and bear arms, I do not have that right in the city where I work, Washington, D.C. There, handguns have been outlawed.

I borrowed a Glock from a co-worker who lived in Virginia, a state with no similar pretense of making itself a gun-free zone. With some help from anti-terrorist experts, I dismantled the gun, stashed the parts in my briefcase, and slipped a couple of bullets into my coat pocket. Then I sailed unimpeded through the metal detector at the Capitol. The guards waved me by as I headed for the nearest rest room to reassemble my weapon.

I had an appointment with Senator Bob Dole, who thought he was going to talk with me about the security threat against the Capitol but had no idea how closely that threat would come to him that day. Midway through the interview, I pulled the gun out of my pocket and laid it on the desk. Then I produced the bullets and handed them to him. It was ridiculously simple. The senator paled briefly but maintained his composure.

He felt obliged to report this breach of security. When he did, both the Capitol police and the D.C. police threatened to arrest me. Neither seemed the slightest bit impressed by my Second Amendment right to keep and bear arms. Equally unimpressed was the Standing Committee of Correspondents, which controls access to the Senate and House press galleries. Even that jury of my peers felt confident they could punish me for carrying a gun. They threatened to take away my congressional press pass until they found out that I hadn't bothered to get one. (I have never thought an American citizen should have to carry a pass to enter the halls of Congress, armed or unarmed.)

In the end, they all backed down to avoid a stink. But I freely concede that the police had every right to arrest me that day. I had carried a gun in a city where one was not allowed, in a city that has become living proof of the NRA bumper sticker that says WHEN GUNS ARE OUTLAWED, ONLY OUTLAWS HAVE GUNS.

Despite the law, there is no shortage of guns in our nation's capital. That is not, however, the fault of any wrong-headed gun ban. There is no shortage of guns because there is no shortage of criminals, because there is no checkpoint at the Potomac River to search people for guns as they come into the city, and because guns are readily available over the counter in nearby Virginia.

I agree that outright gun bans don't work, but we can certainly limit the sale of certain types of unnecessary guns and restrict the legal sale of guns to certain people. Don't count on getting any support from the fanatical minority currently in charge of the NRA, though.

With a great clanking of its crusader's armor, the NRA has risen to defend the Second Amendment above all other rights. This exalted sanction to bear arms, the gun lobby contends, endows citizens with the guns they need to protect their other freedoms.

Statements of support are cited from our Founding Fathers, no less. "What country can preserve its liberties," cited Thomas Jefferson, "if their rulers are not warned from time to time that the people preserve the spirit of resistance? Let them take arms!" Echoed Noah Webster: "The supreme power in America cannot enforce unjust laws by the sword, because the whole body of people are armed." Alexander Hamilton agreed that no standing army could oppress the people while a "large body of citizens . . .

stand ready to defend their own rights."

The Founding Fathers were, after all, revolutionaries who had just won their independence by force of arms. They had bitter reason to be protective of their rights and distrustful of government. The disarming of their fellow citizens would have been unthinkable. Without muskets, they couldn't defend their homes against hostile forces and marauding natives.

But these early Americans had nothing in common with the street gangs and backwoods militias that now hide behind the Second Amendment. Today they pack rapid-fire assault weapons, not antiquated blunderbusses. And they don't protect our liberties, they threaten them.

Our forebears recognized that times would change. They had no intention of imposing their will on future generations. Thomas Jefferson, in particular, made this clear. They may have left us with this odd legacy known as the Second Amendment, but they understood it could become obsolete and so they also left the mechanism to change it. This process, contrary to NRA propaganda, has been at work almost from the day the Second Amendment was adopted. Clearly, the right to keep and bear arms is subject to such limitations as the Congress, state legislatures, and local communities may see fit to impose. Not a single law limiting the right to keep and bear arms has ever been nullified by the courts on Second Amendment grounds. As R. William Ide III, then-president of the American Bar Association, said in 1994, "There is no Second Amendment guarantee. There is no confusion in the law on this issue."

A resolution passed by the House of Delegates of the American Bar Association on firearms violence declared that the right to bear arms, as cited in the Second Amendment, "relates to a 'well regulated militia' and that there are no federal constitutional decisions which preclude regulation of firearms in private hands."

How did they reach that determination when—as we are constantly reminded—the Second Amendment, a part of the Bill of Rights, clearly states that "the right of the people to keep and bear Arms, shall not be infringed?" What could be more plain and forthright? How could anyone fail to see that the Constitution affords every citizen a right that cannot be infringed?

The answer is in the few words the NRA likes to leave out when it propagandizes about the Second Amendment: "A well regulated Militia, being necessary to the security of a free State . . ."

The entire Second Amendment, correctly quoted, reads: "A well regulated Militia, being necessary to the security of a free State, the right of the people to keep and bear Arms, shall not be infringed." Had the Founding Fathers been able to gaze into the future and see the war of words over that sentence, they might have been more specific.

What is a militia? One thing it certainly is *not* is a gang of malcontents and military rejects running around in the woods in camouflage suits. The supreme courts of several states, including Alabama, North Carolina, and Utah, have defined the word *militia*. It is a body of citizens enrolled for discipline as a military force but not engaged in actual service except in emergencies, as distinguished from regular troops or a standing army.

Real militiamen do not show up for training at their convenience. The colonial Minutemen, for example, were required to attend periodic drills. They had to appear regularly for training and discipline and bring with them specified weapons at their own expense. And they were not "citizen volunteers." Every able-bodied man had to appear, or show good cause why he didn't.

No less a figure than George Washington was suspicious of militias. During his presidency he abolished them by, in essence, federalizing them. That is to say, he brought them under direct control of the president. When militiamen resisted the federal government's power to collect a tax on whiskey, Washington sent federal troops to suppress them.

Independent or quasi-independent militias have no status in law and no status in fact.

As the U.S. Court of Appeals for the Third Circuit observed in its 1942 opinion in *United States* v. *Tot,* "[W]eapon bearing was never treated as anything like an absolute right by the common law. It was regulated by statute as to time and place as far back as the Statute of Northampton in 1328 and on many occasions since."

When it comes to interpreting the meaning of the Constitution of the United States, the Supreme Court is the final arbiter, at least for mainstream Americans who accept our system of government. The high court has often addressed the question of how to define a militia and the limitations on the right to keep and bear arms.

As far back as 1886, in a case called *Presser* v. *Illinois,* the Supreme Court ruled on the question of what a militia is. Presser was a member of a Chicago organization called the *Wehr und Lehr Verein.* The *Wehr und Lehr Verein* was, among other things, a private militia that armed its members and trained them to use guns. Private militia were prohibited under Illinois law.

Presser was convicted under that law. He appealed, ultimately to the Supreme Court of the United States, claiming the Second Amendment guaranteed his right to belong to a private militia.

The Supreme Court said it wasn't so: "The citizen of the United States has secured to him the right to keep and bear arms as part of the militia which Congress has the right to organize, and arm, and to drill in companies." That meant Presser's little group of gun-toters was not lawfully organized by Congress.

If the Second Amendment confers the right to keep and bear arms as part of a militia, what about sporting uses, hunting for food, or protecting oneself? Those rights are subject to limitations that may be enacted into law.

To understand what the Second Amendment is driving at, it is necessary to look to Section 10 of Article 1 of the Constitution:

> No State shall, without the Consent of Congress, lay any duty of tonnage, *keep Troops, or Ships of War in time of Peace,* enter into any Agreement or Compact with another State, or with a foreign Power, or engage in War, unless actually invaded, or in such imminent Danger as will not admit of delay. [Emphasis added]

In other words, the states were forbidden to raise their own armies. Yet when the Constitution and Bill of Rights were adopted, most states already had militia laws that required every adult male to arm himself with a suitable musket or rifle and have a supply of powder and ball, a powder horn or similar container, a pouch for the ball, flints, and so forth. And all these citizens were required to assemble periodically on a village green or some similar place to drill.

The Constitution alarmed some people, who feared the consequences if only the federal government were allowed to have an army. Our Founding Fathers were hardened by the fires of revolution, and they knew the dangers of concentrating guns in the hands of a federal army. So a provision was incorporated in the Bill of Rights to guarantee the states the right to organize militias. That is the meaning and purpose of the Second Amendment.

The distinction arises again in what is probably the most important decision that interpreted and applied the Second Amendment. That case, decided in 1939, is *United States* v. *Miller Et Al.* In 1934 the Congress, reacting to the gangster violence of the 1920s and 1930s, enacted the National Firearms Act. It prohibited the transportation in interstate commerce of silencers, fully automatic weapons, and shotguns having barrels less than eighteen inches long or sawed-off shotguns. A man named Jack Miller transported a sawed-off shotgun across state lines, was convicted under the new law, and appealed to the Supreme Court, claiming that Congress was stomping all over his Second Amendment rights.

Sorry, the Court told him, his sawed-off shotgun had nothing to do with a well-regulated militia:

> In the absence of any evidence tending to show that possession or use of a 'shotgun having a barrel of less than eighteen inches in length' at this time has some reasonable relationship to the preservation or efficiency of a well-regulated militia, we cannot say that the Second Amendment guarantees the right to keep and bear such an instrument. Certainly it is not within judicial notice that this weapon is any part of the ordinary military equipment or that its use could contribute to the common defense.

The Supreme Court also said that the obvious purpose of the Second Amendment was "to assure the continuation and render possible the effectiveness of the state militia," and that it "must be interpreted and applied with that end in view."

It is within the discretion of Congress to decide which weapons have "some reasonable relationship to the preservation or efficiency of a well-regulated militia." The point was again made forcefully in 1980 in another case, *Lewis* v. *United States.* The Gun Control Act of 1968 thankfully prohibits felons from owning firearms. Lewis, who had a felony record and a gun, argued with some chutzpah that he was a citizen and that the Second Amendment guaranteed his right to own that gun. The Supreme Court put that wrongheaded notion to rest by saying, "These legislative restrictions on the use of firearms do not trench upon any constitutionally protected liberties."

The Second Amendment is a limitation on the power of Congress—that is, on the power of the federal government. It does not impose a limitation on the states, which are free under the Fourteenth Amendment to enact the laws as local officials see fit. Something that plays well in Peoria may not fly in Fort Lauderdale, and that is the beauty of the Fourteenth Amendment: to localize control of government by the people and make government responsive to differing needs. Thus, Washington, D.C., can ban guns with the approval of the city folks, but Montana or Wyoming would be ill advised to try the same thing.

The right of states to restrict gun ownership as they may see fit was fortified in 1908 in the case of *Twining* v. *State of New Jersey.* In that case the Supreme Court ruled, "The right of trial by jury in civil cases, guaranteed by the Seventh Amendment . . .

and the right to keep and bear arms, guaranteed by the Second Amendment . . . have been distinctly held not to be privileges and immunities of citizens of the United States."

In 1976 Francis J. Warin was convicted of a violation of the Gun Control Act of 1968. He had in his possession an unregistered submachine gun. Warin was an engineer and had made the gun himself. Before the U.S. Court of Appeals for the Sixth Circuit, he floated all the arguments the NRA now customarily makes in defense of its version of the Second Amendment.

He argued that he was a member of the "sedentary militia" of the state of Ohio—that is, the whole body of citizens who could be called into service in an emergency, as distinguished from citizens enrolled in the active militia and required to attend drills. Warin claimed he was entitled to own any weapon that might be used by the armed forces of the United States. It was true that combat soldiers did use 9mm fully automatic weapons. The court rejected his argument, noting that his logic, if followed out, could justify anyone owning an atomic bomb. Warin appealed his case to the Supreme Court, which refused to hear it.

The NRA would like to blame the slate of "anti-gun" decisions by the Supreme Court on liberal justices, particularly those who were members of Chief Justice Earl Warren's court. But none of the crucial decisions I've cited here was made by the Warren court. When the Miller case was decided, Charles Evans Hughes was chief justice. When the Lewis and Warin cases were decided, Warren Burger was chief justice. After his retirement, Chief Justice Burger severely criticized the NRA for insisting on a wholly erroneous and thoroughly discredited view of the Second Amendment.

The late Solicitor General Erwin Griswold summed it up: "Never in history has a federal court invalidated a law regulating the private ownership of firearms on Second Amendment grounds. That the Second Amendment poses no barrier to strong gun laws is perhaps the most well-settled proposition in American constitutional law."

Even legal scholars who believe the Second Amendment may grant some rights—such as the right to keep a firearm under the bed for self-protection—say that such a right could be legally hedged by strict controls. Whatever right the Second Amendment confers, certainly it is not absolute.

In 1993, Connecticut passed a ban on sixty-seven types of assault weapons. On July 24, 1995, the Connecticut Supreme Court upheld the constitutionality of that law. In a unanimous decision, the court held that assault rifles are not essential to self-defense, whereas their use by criminals poses a danger to the police and to society. Chief Justice Ellen Peters wrote, "As long as our citizens have available to them some types of weapons that are adequate reasonably to vindicate the right to bear arms in self-defense, the state may proscribe the use of other weapons."

The moderate, soft-spoken Tanya Metaksa, director of the NRA's lobbying arm, characterized the decision as "bogus on its face."

If it is "bogus," then the courts have been infected with a legal virus that's spreading. The Supreme Court of Ohio upheld a Cleveland ordinance banning assault weapons in that city, and the Supreme Court of Colorado upheld an ordinance banning them in Denver.

The version of the Second Amendment endlessly propagandized by the NRA is a myth and nothing but a myth, pure and simple. The Second Amendment never meant what the NRA says it means. Yet the NRA pounds on this myth, confusing and misinforming its membership. The leadership's stubborn insistence on a wholly discredited idea is silly and would even be amusing except for the fact that it is a lie. Millions of Americans, including many who are not members of the NRA, have come to believe that the Constitution of the United States gives them an unrestricted right to keep and bear arms—any arms. Serious efforts have been made by the NRA's lackeys in Congress to repeal the legislation that denies citizens the right to own machine guns. (Even that is not an absolute prohibition. A citizen may apply for a permit to own a fully automatic weapon.)

Where does the supposed right end? Does the Second Amendment confer the right to own bazookas? Hand-held anti-aircraft missile launchers? Artillery? Atomic bombs? Short only perhaps of atomic bombs, there is a body of people who assert the right to own any of those. The NRA abets them by its propaganda.

Irresponsible myth-making about constitutional rights leads to other harebrained interpretations of the Constitution. For example, a woman asserted in a television interview that her state government had no right to require her to have a driver's license, since that abridged her constitutional right to go where she chose when she chose. And there is a group who solemnly insists that only African Americans are obligated to pay income taxes. For others it is an unconstitutional taking of property, but African Americans must pay because it is compensation to the nation for the confiscation of property caused by their emancipation.

These deluded people differ from NRA members only in that they don't have a multi-million-dollar lobby team in Washington pushing their kooky points of view. The NRA obviously is not responsible for all constitutional delusions, but when it incessantly exhorts the nation to accept its distortion of the Second Amendment, it encourages addled people to put their own spin on the Constitution and find in it a variety of "rights" it does not and never did promise.

If the NRA can rewrite the Constitution to suit its own ideology, why can't others? Why should the courts be the only agencies that can interpret the Constitution? For that matter, why should the Congress, the president, and the courts together have the sole right to apply the Constitution? Why can't private citizens read the Constitution as they see fit and govern themselves accordingly? Why can't we have 250 million idiosyncratic interpretations? Why can't every citizen have his or her own Constitution?

By constantly harping on the theme that the Constitution is under fire, the NRA incites hatred and violence. While insisting that it stands for law and order, the NRA foments anarchy and chaos.

History and constitutional law mean nothing to the current leadership of the NRA. They have their version of the Constitution and seem determined not just to follow it but to impose it on the nation. No one elected them except for a tiny minority of the members of the NRA, the ones who bothered to vote in NRA elections. They have no franchise to amend the Constitution as they see fit. But that is what they seem determined to do: amend by propaganda.

CHAPTER FOUR
U.S. MILITIAS

We Americans are a suspicious bunch, as we surely should be. Our ancestors came here to throw off the shackles of oppressive government. We fiercely guard our right to govern ourselves. We are the sovereigns, and the president and Congress work for us.

It was not easy to secure the adoption of a federal Constitution of the United States. "I smell a rat," said Patrick Henry during the debates in Virginia. Many felt the rights of the states and the rights of the people themselves were being threatened by the establishment of a strong central government. Suspicion of, even hostility to, the federal government has been a constant theme in American history.

What is more, Americans have a long record of resorting to violence to protect their rights. Even before the Revolution, Americans attacked British customs collectors and sometimes tarred and feathered them.

In 1794, when American farmers refused to pay the excise tax on whiskey, insisting the federal government had no right to tax whiskey, President George Washington had to send troops to suppress the Whiskey Rebellion.

New Englanders flouted the embargo imposed by President Thomas Jefferson in an effort to secure America's maritime rights against outrages by the British and French navies.

Americans on the western frontier often simply ignored the law and turned violent against government officers charged with enforcing it. Or, when the sheriff didn't do his job, the citizens did it for him without the niceties of due process.

In 1861, southern states went to war against the government of the United States. Two years later President Abraham Lincoln was compelled to send federal troops to New York City to suppress draft riots at a time when troops were desperately needed at Gettysburg.

Radicals in the labor movement resorted to violence to enforce what they saw as their rights, and business owners turned violent against them in response. Sit-down strikers seized Ford automobile factories and held them. Henry Ford sent thugs to beat up on labor leaders.

During the Great Depression, midwestern farmers resorted to violence to block reluctant sheriffs trying to carry out court-ordered foreclosures.

Hippies called all police officers "pigs" and threw rocks at them. The rocks later became Molotov cocktails.

Presidents Lincoln, Garfield, McKinley, and Kennedy were the victims of assassination by brooding citizens who couldn't get their way in the voting booth. Attempts were made on the lives of Presidents Theodore Roosevelt, Franklin Roosevelt, Harry Truman, Gerald Ford, and Ronald Reagan.

Dr. Martin Luther King, Jr., mounted a nonviolent protest in the name of civil rights; he was murdered. So was Robert Kennedy.

There is a lamentable streak of violence in the American character. It cannot be characterized any other way.

People today talk about their fear of walking the streets of our cities as if it were a twentieth-century development. Hardly. Walking the streets of big cities, particularly at night, particularly on ill-lighted streets with few people, has never been safe—in America or anywhere else. People who found it necessary to move from one place to another on foot at night in the streets of London some two hundred years ago hired torchbearers and armed guards to escort them. The same was true of Paris and other great cities. The streets of American cities in colonial times, or afterward in the nineteenth century, were not safe after dark. The coming of electric street lighting made them safer, but were the streets really safe during the heyday of American gangsters?

Youth gangs and crackheads have made our streets less safe. So has the insistence of the National Rifle Association that everyone has the right to own and to carry just about any weapon he or she chooses.

Freedom to disagree has always been one of our most precious rights. My thoughts are not always your thoughts, but both of us have the right to think as we will. This God-given privilege does not entitle us, however, to implement ideas that trespass on the rights of others.

Freedom is not a license for unrestrained conduct; our right to think and act independently does not transcend our obligations to society. This is the underlying principle on which our democracy is built.

Long ago—less than fifty years after the birth of our nation—

an immigrant named Francis Grund described the America he had discovered: "Few people have so great a respect for the law and are so well able to govern themselves."

Yet a lawless streak has always run through American society, a tendency to carry our freedoms to the extreme and flirt with chaos. Perhaps because of our reluctance to bridle our freedoms, Americans above most other people are addicted to conspiracy theories that run rampant. When bad things happen to good people, it cannot be coincidence or accident; there must be a conspiracy behind it.

The John Birch Society, an ultraconservative organization, used to preach about the Communist conspiracy, telling the American people that such figures as President Dwight D. Eisenhower and General George C. Marshall were "conscious agents of the Communist conspiracy." Of late the Birchers have been abandoned by their decades-long bugaboo and have been obliged to find another one. Today the scarce remnants of the society grumble darkly about a conspiracy mounted by "the Society of the Illuminati," among whose members it says it has discovered Queen Elizabeth II, Henry Kissinger, and the late Nelson Rockefeller.

Today, a distressingly large number of people mumble irrationally about "one worlders," a conspiracy to surrender the Constitution and subject the people of the United States to a world government dominated by the United Nations. To avoid "one-world government," Americans must of course arm themselves and be prepared to conduct guerrilla warfare in the woods and mountains. More about that later.

So there is in the American culture a combustible mix of people:

many habituated to lawlessness and violence, many deluded by conspiracy theories into preparing to defend themselves against conspiracies that are entirely in their imaginations. Add to that a real conspiracy on the part of the NRA to stir this cauldron for its own political agenda and profit, and you have the ingredients for immediate turmoil and future anarchy.

A substantial majority of Americans are troubled by the presence of independent militias and want them investigated. But they are not going to be investigated—not by this Congress—because too many members have been intimidated by their menacing rhetoric.

Who are these militia people, and what do they believe?

It is, of course, impossible to say that every militia member believes this or believes that. Militia members are a widely and wildly varying lot. It is, nevertheless, possible to identify some unifying themes: hatred and suspicion of government, rampant racism, and anti-Semitism.

The following are some of the beliefs commonly held by many militia members.

➤ Agents of the federal government, or of the New World Order, are flying around the country in black helicopters, spying, plotting, and preparing for a United Nations takeover, and trying to blind patriots by shining laser beams into their eyes.

➤ Coded labels have been affixed to highway signs for the purpose of guiding U.N. troops to their objectives.

➤ The government is building detention camps for gun owners.

➤ Foreign troops of various kinds, including Gurkhas and Royal Hong Kong policemen, are training in Montana, preparing for the assault on American liberties.

➤ The federal government, particularly the Clinton administration, has a plan to invade every home in the United States and seize all guns.

➤ Crips, Bloods, and other urban street gangs are being trained to conduct house-to-house searches, looking for guns to confiscate.

➤ Ships and long trains, carrying U.N. military supplies, including Russian and East German equipment, have been spotted in the United States.

➤ The Oklahoma City bomb was set off by the federal government to make people fear and loathe the brave men and women of the militia and justify disarming them. Seismic records show that a bomb exploded inside the Alfred P. Murrah Federal Building seconds before one exploded in a van parked outside. This was done to convince the gullible American public that the bomb in the van killed the victims, whereas in truth they were killed by a government bomb planted inside the building.

➤ An agency of the federal government blew up the building because files were stored there that proved the "truth" about the federal siege of the Branch Davidian complex in Waco, Texas, in 1993.

➤ The Oklahoma City bomb was set off by Japanese agents in retaliation for the Tokyo subway gas attacks, which in turn had been plotted by the CIA in retaliation for Japan's lowering the value of the dollar against the yen.

➤ Chemical spills and other environmental disasters are practice runs for much larger disasters the government will use to drive people out of their homes so U.N. forces can enter their homes and confiscate their weapons.

➤ The Israeli government controls the government of the United States.

➤ Mossad (Israeli intelligence) has so thoroughly penetrated the FBI and the Secret Service that it controls those agencies.

➤ Mossad set off the explosions at the World Trade Center and in Oklahoma City. Its purpose was to increase fear of terrorism in the United States and consequently encourage passage of an anti-terrorist bill advocated by President Clinton.

➤ If an anti-terrorism bill is enacted into law, the FBI will rule the United States as a sort of Gestapo, with of course Mossad controlling the FBI.

➤ The Anti-Defamation League of B'nai B'rith is an Israeli propaganda agency devoted to telling big lies about such subjects as the siege at Waco.

➤ There is a widespread conspiracy to revoke the Constitution of the United States. It will probably be revoked within no more than two years.

➤ The New World Order will implant electronic devices under the skins of all citizens so it can track their activities, maybe even read their thoughts.

➤ The bar codes used on all kinds of products contain sinister secret messages.

➤ The government has developed ways to control the weather and induce earthquakes and floods.

➤ The murder of five children and the wounding of twenty-nine others in a California schoolyard in 1989 by sniper Patrick Purdy was set up by the government, using "mind control" tactics on Purdy, to promote an assault-weapons ban.

➤ The news media are part of the international conspiracy; that's why they refuse to publicize the "information" the militia activists accumulate.

By no means do all militia members accept or endorse such ideas, and these are only a sample of the ideas some members have expressed. Where do people find this hooey? They get it from a variety of sources, but one source on which they rely heavily is a book called *Report From Iron Mountain.* Militia publications frequently quote from this book as an authority for their New World Order notions. It is the blueprint for the New World Order, the master plan for the destruction of the United States.

Report From Iron Mountain begins with an introduction by Leonard C. Lewin, in which he writes that the book was the report of a special study group assembled in an underground bomb shelter in upstate New York in the summer of 1963. The thesis of the study was that permanent peace would be destructive to society, that war provided not only employment but the psychological glue that made citizens obey the law and respect their government. The report set forth a terrifying scenario that the government might act out to provide an alternative to war. Among the things the government might do was create a fictional threat from outer space and mobilize against that nonexistent threat.

The book suggests a variety of tyrannical programs that the government might adopt. Because it purports to be a report from an officially sanctioned think tank, the militia people who pore over it find in it documentary evidence that much of what they fear is true.

But *Report From Iron Mountain* is a hoax. There was no special study group and no think tank to issue the report. Leonard Lewin wrote the whole book himself. When it was published, it was accepted and reviewed as satire. The gullible militia members missed the subtlety of satire. They believe the book and treat it as a bible of their movement.

Copies became scarce, so a few years ago Liberty Lobby, an ultraconservative group, began to reprint the book and sell it. In 1992 the author, Lewin, sued for copyright infringement, and Liberty Lobby replied that if the report was indeed a government document, then it was not subject to copyright law. The case was settled in 1994. The attorney for Liberty Lobby and the founder of that organization himself now admit that Leonard Lewin wrote *Report From Iron Mountain* as a work of fiction.

Another troubling undercurrent in the militia movement is the close relationship between many militia units with racist and anti-Semitic organizations and ideas. Militia spokesmen vehemently deny they are racist or welcome racists into their ranks, but close ties have been detected between many militia organizations and the Ku Klux Klan, Aryan Nation, Posse Comitatus, Christian Identity, and other hate groups.

Affiliations have also developed with violent anti-abortionists. Every citizen is entitled to oppose abortion, but obviously there is no right to attack and kill doctors and nurses, contrary to what many extremist groups have promoted.

Some militia leaders concede there are hate-mongers in their midst—planted there, they charge, by the federal government to damage the reputation of the militia movement and make it less effective.

Let me put this matter in proper perspective: Most militia members are not also affiliated with racist hate groups. But, worrisomely, a growing number are. A notion almost all of them share is that they must take up arms to defend their beliefs. If they decide the government has become oppressive and is interfering with their perceived rights, they believe they are entitled to mount armed attacks on government agents. This is a prescription for anarchy. If every individual has a right to assault lawmen, there can be no government at all. If everyone who turns up in the minority in some democratic decision-making process thinks he or she can overwhelm the majority with a spray of gunfire, society falls apart and nobody has any legal rights.

So, then, who are they?

It is dangerous, of course, to generalize. Militia members can be all kinds of people, and separate units vary widely from one another. Some militia members refer to the members of other militia units as "nuts," "lunatics," and "crackpots" and are vocal about disassociating with them. One militia member, after being told of the Oklahoma City bombing, remarked, "Well, it's about time." Most militia people decry the bombing, though a number of them profess to believe the federal government itself detonated the bomb.

On the whole, people who join militias tend to be small-town or rural citizens. They also tend to be poorly educated. It has always been common for people to loathe and fear what they cannot understand. The statements of militia members betray how little many of them understand. They have one thing in common: obsessive distrust of government, especially of the federal government.

Storyteller Garrison Keillor refers to Lake Wobegon as "the little town that time forgot." There have always been in America some folks whom time apparently forgot. They yearn for a better, simpler era that they imagine existed not so long ago. Never mind that it didn't. Wasn't there a time when you could buy a decent white dress-shirt for one dollar? Yes, there was—about the same time that your entire weekly wages could buy ten of those shirts. Wasn't there a time when you could flush your toilet down a pipe than ran directly to the nearest stream, without some "environmentalist" saying nay? Yes, there was—and you didn't dare swim or fish in that stream.

A better, simpler time. In the 1970s and 1980s, young people used to argue, among other things, that no one needed electrical power generated by atomic power plants. Some of them talked about retreating to their own version of Walden Pond and living a gentle, simple life. They had to be reminded that there are not enough Walden Ponds in the world to afford that idyllic, uncomplicated life for everyone.

The militia men and women have a simplistic idea that the social and economic problems of the world will go away if they just resist government efforts to solve those problems.

Citizens of Idaho visit New York City, see the South Bronx, and recoil in horror. They wouldn't want to live there. No, neither would I, nor would most of the people who already live there. What would happen if the beleaguered populace of the South Bronx and, say, Watts decided they could live a better life in Idaho and moved there by the hundreds of thousands?

The point is, city people exist. Non-Christians exist. Non-whites exist. Do the militia people think they can exterminate them? The majority of Americans do not live in a mountain paradise. They live in towns and cities where social and environmental concerns dictate the conditions of their lives, and where the laws that have been adopted to improve conditions are not dictatorial and do not represent an assault on anyone's liberties.

The militia people are simply out of touch with reality, which, unfortunately, does not discourage some of them from plotting maniacal assaults on law and order.

What do they do?

My peers, the news media, generally have created an image of a lot of camouflage-clad, middle-aged, overweight, befuddled used-car salesmen and insurance agents and their wives huffing and puffing around in the woods, playing at "military training." More to be pitied than censured. More comic than dangerous.

Some fit this harmless stereotype. But some have demonstrated themselves to be ominously dangerous.

➤ In Indiana, a gang of militia members blocked the enforcement of a child-custody order.

➤ In Montana, a local official was threatened by an armed militia gang when he tried to arrest a woman for a traffic violation.

➤ A man with militia ties allegedly shot a Missouri highway patrolman to avenge the arrest of another militia member.

➤ Members of a Montana "patriot" movement threatened to blow up part of the regional electric power transmission system, causing utilities in fifteen western states to go on alert.

➤ A Tampa "patriot" group has established what it calls a "constitutional court." It ordered four judges, the tax collector, and several other county officials to submit to "arrest" and stand "trial" before this court. The man and woman who set up the court are reported to have said that militia volunteers would enforce the orders of the court.

➤ Two Minnesota members of what is called the Minnesota Patriots Council have been convicted of a conspiracy to kill federal agents with a deadly biological poison.

➤ Members of a Virginia militia group have been charged with stockpiling machine guns. Investigators discovered that they planned to raid a National Guard armory to obtain more guns. The following, taken from a computer disk found by federal agents, is what they were about to issue in their newsletter:

> Hit and run tactics will be our method of fighting. . . . We will destroy targets such as telephone relay centers, bridges, fuel storage tanks, communications towers, radio stations, airports, etc. . . . Human targets will be engaged when it is beneficial to the cause to

eliminate particular individuals who oppose us (troops, police, political figures, snitches, etc.).

➤ The Militia of Montana is one of the most extreme militia, or "patriot," groups in America. It has published a pamphlet entitled *The Militia*, in which it says the following:

> To balance the military power of the nation with the might of the militia will put at odds any scheme by government officials to use the force of government against the people. Therefore, when the codes and statutes are unjust for the majority of the people, the people will rightly revolt and the government will have to acquiesce without a shot being fired, because the militia stands vigilant in carrying out the will of the people in defense of rights, liberty and freedom.
>
> The purpose of government is in the protection of the rights of the people, and when it does not accomplish this, the militia is the crusader who steps forward, and upon it rests the mantle of the rights of the people.

➤ At a "Constitution Restoration" meeting held in Lakeland, Florida, in the fall of 1994, a flyer was distributed to the thousand or so people who attended. It said, "A strong and growing Underground Patriotic Movement with state-wide militia groups exists against the Sinister Ones that is unreported by the monopolistic and controlled establishment media."

The flyer identified the "Sinister Ones" as the House of Rothschild, international bankers, the Federal Reserve System, the Trilateral Commission, and others. "What is the range of British and Israeli influence in the upper tiers?" it asked. It urged readers to "stockpile food, water, guns and ammo." It asked all gun owners to fire a "warning shot" at 11:00 P.M. on November 11, 1994, as a signal to Congress. "Congress is forcing the country into a civil war," the flyer stated.

➤ A militia organizer in Idaho told members, "Go and look your legislator in the face, because someday you may be forced to blow it off."

Some people in communities where militias are conspicuous live in fear of them. A resident of Noxon, Montana, headquarters of the Militia of Montana, had this to say to a writer for the *Seattle Post-Intelligencer:* "There's a real fear of these people. They have guns. They have missiles. They're not someone to play with. They're really not. Please don't say who I am."

Other people have told stories of economic pressure brought to bear on them by the militia, of being driven out of business by militia hostility. Some people have simply picked up and moved away from their hometown, driven out by threats. The threats vary but usually involve physical violence against a person or a family. Here and there, a law enforcement officer admits to being intimidated by militia members.

Not all militia members act this way or sympathize with those who do. A great majority of those affiliated with militia organizations in the past were sincere in their commitment to nonviolence, at least until the day that the New World Order police invade their homes. But since New World Order police are figments of their own imagination, no confrontation with them has ever been possible, so the majority of militia members are essentially harmless. They are play-acting in a dire but silly drama. Meanwhile, however, their organizations are stockpiling weapons that a minority are prepared to use.

Incredibly, the militias have supporters in Congress. One is freshman Representative Helen Chenoweth of Idaho, the recipient of a $4,950 campaign contribution from the NRA Political Victory Fund. After the Oklahoma City bombing, she acknowledged that "violent acts like that cannot be condoned and must be punished" but contended that "we still must begin to look at the public policies that may be pushing people too far."

She also buys the stories of roving flights of mysterious black helicopters spying on the citizenry. In February 1995, she issued a news release condemning the supposed flights and warning government officials that she would become their "worst nightmare" unless the black helicopter flights ceased.

She has pledged herself to seek legislation that would require federal law-enforcement officers to obtain written permission from local sheriffs to carry firearms in their counties. "They shouldn't be armed unless they're deputized by the local sheriff," she says.

Videotapes of Chenoweth's speeches are sold at meetings of the Militia of Montana. One Idaho newspaper has suggested that Helen Chenoweth has become a militia "poster child."

House Speaker Newt Gingrich has defended Chenoweth's rhetoric, saying, "There is in rural America a genuine fear of the federal government and of Washington, D.C., as a place that doesn't understand their way of life and doesn't understand their values."

Yet all told, 1995 was a bad year for the militias. Already exposed in the news media, already the subject of suspicion by the majority of Americans, they suffered hugely from the Oklahoma

City bombing. A Yankelovich poll in April showed that 80 percent of Americans thought the militias were dangerous, 63 percent thought they were a threat to our way of life, 55 percent thought they were crazy, and only 21 percent thought they were patriots. Confirming the militias' worst fears, 68 percent thought the federal government should spy on the militias and monitor their activities.

At this writing, the actual connection between the militias and the alleged Oklahoma City bomber, Timothy McVeigh, is tenuous. Still, most Americans are inclined to believe that when people play with guns and talk insane conspiracy notions, monumental violence is bound to happen. Whether McVeigh is guilty or not, someone is, and that someone is conspicuously not the government. It is hard to escape the conclusion that conspiracy preachments contributed to the mind-set that exploded the bomb. The sincere disclaimers by militia leaders have not allayed the hostility and suspicion with which militias are now viewed.

Businesspeople who joined militia units in the belief they were patriotic groups have quit in large numbers, now believing they cannot afford to be identified with, as one ex-member put it, "gun-toting, paranoid fanatics."

On May 5, 1995, President Clinton publicly denounced the militias in a televised speech originating in Michigan. "There is nothing patriotic about hating your country," he said. "How dare you call yourselves patriots and heroes? . . . If you say violence is an acceptable way to make change, you are wrong. . . . If you appropriate our sacred symbols for paranoid purposes and compare yourselves to colonial militias, you are wrong."

His speech struck a chord. In many communities, people who had looked at the local militia unit with amused tolerance, as well as those who had kept their silence because they were afraid, began to complain and condemn.

The result, according to my sources, has been a diminution of militia membership. As opposed to popular belief about militia growth, many members have quit. Militia units have disbanded. Some of them, with somber drama, have dramatically destroyed their records. Before the Oklahoma City bombing, it was estimated that militia membership nationwide did not exceed 100,000. We have no numbers—most militia units won't talk about numbers—but it is likely the number has been much reduced.

Steven L. Gardner, research director of the Coalition for Human Dignity, a watchdog group that tracks militias, says, "While the movement has not been proven criminally responsible for the [Oklahoma City] bombing, it has been indicted morally. For some, the cost of being associated with such a stigma is too high. . . . We are seeing weekend warriors . . . distancing themselves from the hard cores, the true ideologues of the movement."

These true ideologues have not been tamed by the Oklahoma bombing. A leader of the Oregon Militia said, "If they would blow up one of their own buildings, who knows what they could do to militias."

The alarming result has undoubtedly been the consolidation of hard-core believers. Most of the moderates have left. What remains is a kernel of grim extremists—the fanatic fringe—and they are dangerous. Some of them claim they have disbanded because they learned they were being infiltrated by federal informers. Others say they disbanded because they feared an imminent attack by federal officers, perhaps even troops. And some say they have only appeared to disband, that in fact they have gone underground or have broken up into smaller units.

So what does the NRA have to do with militias? Is this just an exercise in guilty-by-association? The organization denies any official connection with any militia unit. On November 10, 1994, it issued this statement:

> The Board of Directors of the National Rifle Association has not adopted a formal policy regarding the formation of citizen militia groups, such as has occurred in numerous states. . . . Although the NRA has not been involved in the formation of any citizen militia units, neither has the NRA discouraged, nor would the NRA contemplate discouraging, exercise of any constitutional right. . . .
>
> It is the NRA's view, based on law . . . that all able bodied persons, explicitly those between the ages of 17 and 45, are members of the Federal unorganized militia . . . the individual right to own firearms is guaranteed by the Constitution, but the right to own firearms is not at all dependent upon the militia clause. The militia clause of the Second Amendment merely adds to the reason for the right, which is a common law right rooted in the right of protection of self, family, and community.

An NRA leaflet distributed at its 1995 convention declared, "It is time to stop worrying . . . about black helicopters and U.N. invaders and focus on voting out of office those who would deny . . . [gun owners' rights]. . . . Gun owners . . . cannot afford to waste their resources on flights of fancy."

The NRA's executive vice president, Wayne LaPierre, told the convention: "NRA patriots are being confused with Grade

A terrorists. We don't fight with bullets but with ballots. . . . There's no one in the NRA who supports or fantasizes about terrorism, insurrection, or treason."

Thus, after the Oklahoma City bombing, the NRA made a conscious effort to distance itself from the militias. Even so, the relationship between militia people and the NRA is more intimate than the NRA would like to admit. A large number of militia members are also NRA members. Since those people tend to be activists at best, paranoid fanatics at worst, they attend NRA meetings and vote in NRA elections.

There is a national network of gun shows, a network that was actively pursued by Timothy McVeigh. At a typical gun show, militia members mill around in their clown suits staring at weapon displays and browsing through racist and anti-Semitic pamphlets and books. At most of these shows the NRA has a recruitment booth.

Two months before the Oklahoma City bombing, the NRA's Tanya Metaksa traveled to Lansing, Michigan, to meet with leaders of the Michigan Militia. One of the militia leaders present was Ken Adams. He said it was the NRA that asked for the meeting, adding, "A lot of our members are their members, of course, and we wanted to formalize how we would work together."

The NRA may want to disassociate itself with the militia movement, but it named Sheriff Richard Mack of Arizona its Law Enforcement Officer of the Year at its 1995 annual meeting in Phoenix. "People get all upset when they hear about militias," said Sheriff Mack, "but what's wrong with it? . . . I wouldn't hesitate for a minute to call out my posse against the federal government if it gets out of hand." The NRA has given Sheriff Mack $25,000 from its legal defense fund to help him maintain a lawsuit challenging the constitutionality of the Brady Law.

What responsibility, if any, does the NRA have for the violence committed or threatened by militias?

Dennis Henigan, director of the Legal Action Project of the Center to Prevent Handgun Violence, charges that the NRA actively encourages the militia movement as one of its fund-raising strategies. He says:

> The NRA has pushed an interpretation of the Second Amendment that . . . is ultimately about resistance to tyrannical government. The militia and other groups are acting that out, engaging in dissent through armed force. The idea is that if you don't like abortion clinics, shoot doctors. If you don't like the ATF, blow up a building. Obviously the NRA will not say this in such blunt terms, but it's the logical extension to what they've been saying for years.

In his infamous "jack-booted thugs" letter, LaPierre wrote:

> Most Americans don't realize that our freedoms are slowly slipping away. They don't understand that politicians and bureaucrats are chipping away at the American way of life. . . . <u>Unless we take action today, the long slide down the slippery slope will only continue until there's no freedom left in America at all</u>. . . . This, the battle we're fighting today . . . is a battle to retake the most precious, most sacred ground on earth. This is a battle for freedom.

This same letter to the NRA membership also implored, "<u>I need you to make a special contribution to the NRA of $15, $20,</u>

$25, $35, $50 or the most generous amount you can afford."
[LaPierre's emphasis throughout]

Strong rhetoric. Incendiary words. What impact does such language have on the gullible? Some were sufficiently lured to send the money LaPierre asked for.

Timothy McVeigh was a member of the NRA for at least four years. That means he received an NRA magazine and NRA mailings and was bombarded with this kind of invective. Maybe it had no impact on him. In 1992, McVeigh wrote the following letter to his congressman:

> Recently I saw an article in the *Buffalo News* that detailed a man's arrest, one of the charges being "possession of a noxious substance (CS gas)." This struck my curiosity [sic], so I went to the New York State Penal Law. Sure enough, section 270 prohibits possession of any noxious substance, and included in section 265 is a ban on the use of "stun guns." Now I am male and fully capable of physically defending myself, but how about a female?
>
> I strongly believe in a God-given right to self-defense. Should any other person or governing body be able to tell another person that he/she cannot save their own life, because it would be a violation of a law? In this case, which is more important: faced with a rapist/murderer, would you pick a.) to die, a law-abiding citizen or b.) live and go to jail?
>
> It is a lie if we tell ourselves that the police can protect us everywhere, at all times. I am in shock that a law exists which denies a woman's right to self-defense. Firearms restrictions are bad enough, but now a woman can't even carry Mace in her purse?

On the back of the envelope in which this letter was sent was a stamp with a bald eagle and the words I'M THE NRA.

On the one hand, obviously the NRA did not inspire Timothy McVeigh to commit the horrible crime he has been charged with. On the other hand, can the NRA evade all responsibility if its invective influences susceptible personalities to act out their violent fantasies?

What about the none-too-bright and none-too-well-informed men and women who are attracted to the militia movement? Some of them stalk agents of the Bureau of Alcohol, Tobacco and Firearms. The FBI reports that it has had to relocate some of its agents because of death threats against them and their families. Michigan Militia members have been found with the names and addresses of BATF agents and the addresses of their children's schools. Just what do they have in mind?

Can the NRA disassociate itself entirely from militia men and women who commit violent acts or scheme to commit them? Can an organization that distributes vitriolic language in mass mailings absolve itself from all responsibility if some people heed its call to arms?

CHAPTER FIVE

THE BELEAGUERED BRADY BILL

On March 30, 1981, John W. Hinckley, Jr., staked out a Washington, D.C., hotel and waited for the president of the United States to emerge. Folded in Hinckley's palm was a .22-caliber pistol he had purchased in a Dallas pawnshop five months earlier. Hinckley had plunked down just $29 for this Saturday-night special. The bullets in the chamber were nicknamed "Devastators."

When Ronald Reagan and his entourage stepped out onto the sidewalk, Hinckley began firing. A ricocheting bullet seriously wounded the president but failed to kill him. As Secret Service agents shoved the president into a waiting limousine, three in the entourage lay grievously wounded on the ground. The worst injury was suffered by James Brady, the forty-year-old presidential press secretary, who was struck in the forehead. The Devastator, designed to explode on impact, did not, but it still lived up to its name. It devastated the lives of James Brady and his wife, Sarah. Jim Brady survived but suffered extensive brain damage. The NRA leadership didn't know it at the time, but they had just acquired a potent enemy.

In 1982, a small organization called Handgun Control, Inc., contacted Sarah Brady and asked her to speak in California in favor of Proposition 15, a ballot initiative that would have banned the sale of handguns in California while allowing existing handgun owners to keep their weapons. At that time, her husband was still a staff member of the Reagan administration, the president was opposed to gun control, and Sarah felt it would be inappropriate for her to endorse Prop 15. She declined.

Three years later, Sarah Brady had a frightening experience. While riding in a friend's pickup truck, her six-year-old son found a pistol. He thought it was a toy and playfully pointed it at his mother. She thought it was a toy too, but when she took it from him she discovered it was a loaded .22-caliber revolver. Back in Washington, she learned that Congress was about to pass a bill strongly lobbied for by the NRA, called the McClure-Volkmer Bill. McClure-Volkmer was meant to roll back such federal gun control as existed. Sarah Brady was shocked that anyone would even consider such a bill.

It was then that she called Handgun Control and asked if they still needed her help. In no time she was a board member of the group and its chief spokesperson. Although McClure-Volkmer became law, a few of its most extreme provisions, including one that would have made it easier to sell handguns, had been amended out. Sarah Brady's persuasive guest editorials in newspapers and appearances before congressional committees, as well as her frequent appearances on TV talk shows, were given generous credit for watering down the bill. It made her the worst kind of villain to the NRA, which immediately began to undermine her in every possible way.

In 1987 Handgun Control decided to focus its efforts on one piece of legislation, the bill that was to become known as the Brady Bill. By any reasonable standard, the Brady Bill is an innocuous piece of legislation. It requires a five-day waiting period for a person wishing to buy a handgun. The point is to give local police a chance to check out that person before the gun is delivered. If the would-be buyer has a felony record—has been convicted of committing a serious crime—or has a history of mental illness, he or she cannot buy the handgun.

The authors of the bill knew it wasn't a no-fault solution to gun violence. As the NRA has repeatedly pointed out, John Hinckley owned two other handguns, which he had bought in California where there is a fifteen-day waiting period. At the time he had no felony record or history of mental illness.

But if the Brady Bill has saved even one life, it has been worthwhile. In fact, it has saved many more than one by forcing angry, embittered, or suicidal people to wait five days before they can have their guns.

So moderate was the premise behind the Brady Bill that as recently as the 1970s even the NRA did not oppose a waiting period. Why, then, did the group fight so angrily and tenaciously against the Brady Bill?

One reason is that the NRA, once an organization of sportsmen, is now an ambitious political machine with a rigid agenda and a determination to make its agenda public policy for the United States.

Another reason is that the leadership, not necessarily the membership, of the NRA now takes an utterly intransigent position relative to gun control, any gun control, no matter how limited or beneficial. The NRA position is that any gun control is simply a crack in the wall to be followed inevitably by the banning of all gun ownership. The current leadership of the NRA cannot be characterized as anything but gun fanatics. Theirs is an in-your-face, no-holds-barred, take-no-prisoners attitude.

To the present leadership of the NRA, there is no such thing as compromise, no such thing as reasonable or limited gun control. What is more, you are either "fer us or agin us." The NRA has friends and enemies, nothing else. To be a "friend," you must accept every element of their dogma. The slightest deviation makes you an enemy.

Speaking on ABC's *Nightline* on May 1, 1995, a former NRA board member had this to say: "The old NRA was willing to sit down with legislators and discuss things, and perhaps bring out legislation that would accomplish the desired objective without being overly restrictive. And the new NRA goes in with a no-compromise attitude: 'You vote the way we want you to vote or we're gonna get you in the next election.'"

President Reagan was, throughout his presidency, a powerful ally of those who believe in the right to own firearms. But on March 28, 1991, he spoke at the George Washington University Medical Center, where his gunshot wound from Hinckley's bullet had been treated ten years earlier. His words deeply hurt the NRA hard-liners and were heard nationwide on that evening's TV news shows: "You do know that I'm a member of the National Rifle Association, and my position on the right to bear arms is well known. But I want you to know something else, and I am going to say it in clear, unmistakable language: I support the Brady Bill and I urge the Congress to enact it without further delay."

The NRA leadership was stunned. Several of the most prominent officers said the venerable stalwart of conservative causes had taken leave of his senses. One of them said he doubted President Reagan had any idea what was in the bill. Tanya Metaksa, then an NRA board member, publicly said she "felt somebody had stabbed me in the back." Because of Reagan's statement, a man who had been a hero to the NRA suddenly became a pariah.

The right to keep and bear arms is constantly referred to by the NRA as "a sacred right." It follows, to pursue their logic, that defense of this right is a religious duty. To them, the right to keep and bear arms is the most important right afforded by the Bill of Rights, because all the others depend on this one. The people will use their arms in defense of their other rights.

Against whom? In the past it was against the Soviet Union, which some believed surely would invade our country sooner or later, defeat our armed forces, and leave American liberties to be protected only by nail-tough citizens in the hills with their rifles and pistols. The end of the Cold War terminated this fantasy. Against whom, now, will the stalwarts fight? Against the government, of course. Against the Bureau of Alcohol, Tobacco and Firearms, which has the temerity to enforce such gun-control laws as the United States has. Against the FBI perhaps. Maybe against the IRS. Against any law enforcement agency or officer, federal, state, or local, that the stalwarts perceive as violating their real or imagined rights.

Also, of course, against the criminals in the streets.

It is easy for the NRA to win over the faintly addled members of militias. But entirely rational citizens do not require preachments from the NRA to encourage them to arm themselves in their homes, to protect themselves against what may happen before the police arrive. We can call 911, but what do we do in the long minutes before the police can get there?

The Brady Bill had nothing to do with that question. Or, for that matter, with fleeing to the hills to fortify ourselves against the Red Army or the assault forces of the BATF. A handgun purchased after a five-day waiting period would be just as effective as one bought on impulse.

Why, then, the fanatical opposition to the Brady Bill?

An element of the problem is that the present leadership of the NRA takes an apocalyptic view of gun control. In their political propaganda, every struggle to enact or to defeat the least and most insignificant limitation on arms importation or sales or possession signals Armageddon.

Reasonable people in Congress, in the population at large, or, for that matter, in the membership of the NRA, might say, "The Brady Bill is a reasonable restraint that does not threaten our right to keep and bear arms." But such a rational position is anathema to the NRA leadership. To them a concession, no matter how slight, is the first step on the way to what they call "the disarming of America."

To the NRA leadership there is no distinction between reasonable and limited restrictions on gun purchase and ownership on the one hand, and confiscation of all the arms owned by the American people on the other. The NRA is worried about the occasional congressman and rare senator who would like to see a total ban on handgun ownership. No need for panic. Only a small minority of the American people feel the same way. A gun can be found in nearly half of American households.

There are those for whom a gun is an abhorrent tool with no practical use. A friend of mine moved from the Midwest to the Northeast. When he mentioned to new friends that he owned three handguns, a shotgun, and a muzzle-loading rifle, some of them were shocked. They had never touched a gun and were dismayed to hear that he kept such things in his home. But in most of the country, it is an odd household that does not have at least one gun somewhere in the house.

Only a small minority of Americans favor a ban on handguns, and only a tiny minority favor any limitations at all on long guns, except "assault rifles." So the "vigilance" against outright gun bans, for which the NRA constantly takes credit, is a sham. With or without the NRA, a handgun ban would not pass through Congress in this century or the first half of the next. A rifle/shotgun ban has no chance at all. If the NRA ceased to exist tomorrow, the right of the people to keep and bear arms would be completely secure.

So how does the NRA justify its existence? By fighting legislation like the Brady Bill, which is aimed at stopping felons and insane people from getting their hands on guns, and by making each of those bills seem like the first step on the road to tyranny.

How does the NRA do it? By buying influence in Washington. According to reports filed with the Federal Election Commission, in the 1993–1994 election cycle, the NRA contributed $1,442,519 to Republican candidates and $410,519 to Democratic candidates. That money did not come directly from the National Rifle Association but from an affiliated entity called the NRA Political Victory Fund. The money, just the same, flows from the NRA's unrelenting fund-raising efforts.

The NRA does not limit itself to contributing money to candidates. It buys ads, distributes literature, and runs TV spots to elect the men and women it wants and defeat those it does not. The money it spends this way is in addition to outright contributions to campaigns—contributions that are limited by law.

Some of the contributions pay off; some of them go down a dry well. Among the recipients of the NRA's largest contributions were Congressman Roscoe Bartlett of Maryland, and Texas senator Kay Bailey Hutchinson, both winners in 1994. NRA support failed to win election for Ben Clayburgh in North Dakota or Oliver North in Virginia, however.

No one has ever accused the NRA of restraint or timidity. In its political ads, it goes for the jugular. Those who can't be bought are scorned. One of the NRA's sworn enemies is Congressman Charles Schumer, a Democrat representing the Tenth District of New York. Above a picture of him in NRA publications, a headline reads MEET THE CRIMINAL'S CONGRESSMAN. A part of the statement about him reads: "His consistent anti-gun record makes him the criminal's best friend in Congress."

The NRA constantly urges its members to "bury Congress in mail, deafen it with phone calls," and a significant number of its members do write and call. The NRA does not deny that it means to intimidate members of Congress. Any member who offered even minimal support for the Brady Bill knew he or she would be targeted for retaliation.

The bill was repeatedly defeated in Congress between the years 1987 and 1993. This in spite of the fact that public opinion polls showed that a vast majority of the American public favored it, and in spite of the fact that a substantial majority of representatives and senators at least privately hoped to see it pass.

These defeats were accomplished by cynical manipulation on the part of the NRA lobbyists. They knew legislative procedure far better than did the less experienced lobbyists of Handgun Control, Inc. Among the NRA ploys was to offer substitute bills, heeding the legislative cliché that you can beat something with something easier than beat something with nothing.

Their favorite anti-Brady gambit was a substitute that would have mandated the establishment of a nationwide computer database that police departments could check instantly, thus eliminating the need for a waiting period. The fact that such a database was impractical and would have required five to ten years to establish was blithely overlooked.

Even when the Brady Bill finally passed both houses, it did not become law, because President George Bush insisted that he would sign it only if it were part of a comprehensive anti-crime law. It was duly incorporated in an anti-crime bill, but that bill also failed in the Senate after Bush threatened to veto it because it was too "soft on crime." Bush himself didn't have the political courage to stand up to the NRA until after the "jack-booted thugs" letter, when he was no longer president and no longer needed to curry anyone's favor.

Candidate Bill Clinton promised to sign the Brady Bill if it was enacted and sent to him. It did finally pass, despite last-ditch efforts of the NRA to derail it; and he did sign it. It is now the Brady Law, and the focus of a determined effort of Republicans in the 104th Congress to repeal it.

So how has it worked? The NRA characterizes it as a failure.

On March 5, 1995, the *Atlanta Journal and Constitution* reported:

> The NRA and its members believe there's a plot to take their guns away to make way for a dictatorship. They equate those who advocate any type of gun control to Nazis, saying that Hitler's first step was gun control. But there's another reason their hatred for the ATF has recently intensified. They can't stand that the Brady Law is a raving success. By February 1995, some 41,000 criminals have been stopped from purchasing handguns. In 30 localities alone, 4,365 were convicted felons, 649 were illegal drug users, 63 were under a domestic violence restraining order. These statistics come from a survey of law enforcement agencies across the country, large and small, rural and urban.

The Fraternal Order of Police confirms the strong trend, although their specific numbers vary from those cited above.

A Connecticut law enacted in 1994 and not entirely in effect until 1995 requires a background check for handgun purchasers, and that they pass a test demonstrating they know how to use such weapons safely. The check-and-test process takes about two and a half months. A survey of local chiefs of police shows that crimes involving handguns have dropped 20 percent since the law has been in effect.

As of February 1995, only ten federal prosecutions had been instituted under the Brady Law. The NRA immediately jumped on this statistic as proof that the law is useless. Spokespersons for the BATF explained, however, that the purpose of the Brady Law is to prevent gun sales to felons and the emotionally disturbed, not to institute thousands of prosecutions.

The NRA had not spoken its final word on the subject of the Brady Bill. It made repeal a priority element of its agenda in the new Republican Congress that took office in January 1995. As of this writing, the NRA has not succeeded.

The NRA's influence on Congress continues to be pernicious. In June 1995, the House Judiciary Committee dropped a ban on "cop killer" bullets, the ones designed to pierce the body armor worn by many police officers.

A true bulletproof vest consists of steel plates and can weigh more than fifty pounds. No police officer can go about his daily work wearing such armor. They put them on for special situations only. Many thousands of police officers do wear, all the time they are on duty, vests made of several plastics that will stop nearly all slugs. These vests have saved thousands of police lives.

In 1986 Congress enacted a law, which was signed by President Reagan, banning metal bullets meant to penetrate these vests. Recently it has been discovered that plastic bullets can be made to penetrate them too. Representative Charles Schumer introduced an amendment to President Clinton's anti-terrorism bill to ban plastic cop-killer bullets too. On June 14, 1995, the House Judiciary Committee voted, 16 to 14, to ban any bullet, of whatever material made, capable of penetrating armor vests.

Two freshman Republicans joined Democrats in supporting the ban. Neal Knox, a board member of the NRA and considered by many to be its most influential officer, said the two Republicans had voted that way because they "didn't know any better."

The next day the vote was reconsidered, the two freshmen Republicans reversed themselves, and the broader ban on cop-killer bullets was dead. Why? How could anyone oppose such a reasonable limitation on ammunition? Who needs a cop-killer bullet?

"If a bullet can rip through a bulletproof vest like a knife through hot butter, then it ought to be history," said President Clinton. "We should ban it." Speaking to a group of hunters, he said, "I have never seen a deer, a duck, or a wild turkey wearing a Kevlar vest. You don't need these bullets."

So what reason could there be for opposing a ban on armor-piercing bullets? The NRA found reason in its ideological fear and loathing of any limitation on guns or ammunition. Wayne LaPierre explained, "Bill Clinton wants the Treasury Department to ban any ammunition that will penetrate Kevlar, which includes virtually any hunter's ammunition. So it's basically an ammunition ban, in a back door way."

There seems to be no end to the fanaticism of the current leadership of the NRA. By this action and others like it, they have won the general hostility of the nation's police organizations, which used to work in cooperation with the NRA.

In July of 1995, the NRA took one defeat in Congress. It had supported a bill to restore the gun rights of convicted felons if they paid for background checks. In point of fact, such a program existed prior to 1992, and Congress refused to fund it any longer. During the period when it was in effect, many violent felons were allowed to rearm, and some of them were convicted of new crimes. President Clinton spoke out against renewing the practice. So did the Fraternal Order of Police. "The gun lobby's radicalism apparently knows no bounds," said Senator Frank Lautenberg. "The new majority in Congress is willing to do almost anything on their behalf."

Well, not everything, as it turned out. The House Appropriations Committee rejected the bill. "Today the Appropriations Committee stood up to the National Rifle Association," said Congressman Edward J. Markey, who had led the effort to defeat the bill. "That the NRA should have wanted even convicted felons to be able to buy handguns demonstrates how it places its ideology above all reason and above the public interest."

CHAPTER SIX
BASHING THE BATF

No less an authority on propaganda than Adolf Hitler had some wisdom that the National Rifle Association has taken to heart: "Propaganda must not serve the truth, especially insofar as it might bring out something favorable for the opponent."

It is further a principle of propaganda that if you repeat that big lie often enough and shout it loudly enough, gradually you will win some people over to believing it. Thus, it isn't enough to call a federal officer who enforces gun laws "incompetent" or "wrong." You must shout something more attention-getting—for example, "jack-booted thug!"

Strident causes thrive more heartily if they have one of two things going for them: a martyr to the cause or an enemy of the cause. When unfettered firearms are your cause, martyrs are more likely to be found in the opposing camp. That leaves the NRA in need of a deadly enemy. Meet the Bureau of Alcohol, Tobacco and Firearms (aka the "jack-booted thugs").

The BATF, an agency of the Treasury Department, is charged with enforcing federal firearms laws. Because it has the temerity to do just that, it has become the whipping boy of the NRA, which is determined to see the BATF abolished.

The BATF is an agency that shoots itself in the foot often enough to make it a limping target for critics. But the NRA conveniently ignores the excellent law enforcement work the BATF does on many fronts—work that has been commended by many state and local police departments.

The NRA has recruited a number of members of Congress to sponsor legislation to make the BATF disappear. So rabid is NRA hatred of the BATF that the gun lobby actually lined up some of its slave senators to sponsor a bill designed to strip BATF agents of their retirement benefits.

This is nothing new. In 1980 Ronald Reagan had the strong support of the NRA in his first campaign for president. He promised to abolish the BATF. In fact, he tried. But the NRA had overlooked the fact that no federal agency ever really goes away. When the NRA discovered that the BATF functions would be transferred to the FBI and the Secret Service—agencies with sophisticated computer capability—the gun lobby concluded it would far rather have a poorly equipped BATF enforcing gun laws and withdrew its demand for abolition. Under NRA prodding, the Congress had already cut BATF appropriations for computer equipment and forbade it to establish a computerized national gun registry system.

The NRA's Wayne LaPierre reached a new level of hysteria and vilification of the BATF in 1995 with his "jack-booted thugs" comment.

About the same time that the LaPierre letter went out, the NRA began publishing rabidly intemperate ads critical of the

BATF. One of them declared, "Tell the Clinton White House to Stay Out of Your House." The ad featured two men in supposed BATF uniforms carrying 9mm carbines. The lengthy text pictured the BATF as a Gestapo-like agency that regularly bursts into people's homes to threaten and harass them, even assault them. It spoke of a "reign of storm-trooper tactics" and warned darkly that the recently enacted assault-weapons ban would broaden the BATF's "tyrannical record."

Undersecretary of the Treasury Ronald K. Noble wrote to Tanya Metaksa:

> The advertisement alludes darkly to ATF's "threat[s] to civil liberties," "contempt for civil rights," and a "tyrannical record of misconduct and abuse of power." Allow me to provide the truth about ATF's record. Of the over 10,000 search warrants served by ATF agents in the last decade, not one has led to any civil court to render any adverse judgments for constitutional violations. Not one.
>
> While the NRA spends lavishly on ads to fight ATF, ATF agents put their lives on the line to protect our communities and our citizens' property from armed criminals. Since 1986, the more than 6,000 armed career criminals and armed drug traffickers ATF brought to justice have been sentenced to more than 55,000 years in prison. Taking these felons off our streets has, by some estimates, prevented over 4 million crimes and saved countless lives and dollars. ATF agents make America safer.

Reaction from the nation's police agencies was swift and strong. The Secret Service rescinded the NRA's invitation to participate in its annual shooting competition for law enforcement officers.

John T. Whetsel, president of the International Association of Chiefs of Police (IACP), wrote a letter to the *Washington Post*, protesting the newspaper's publication of the ad. He said, "I was appalled by the outrageous advertisement carried in your newspaper yesterday, urging citizens to 'Tell the Clinton White House to Stay Out of Your House' and attacking the Bureau of Alcohol, Tobacco and Firearms. . . . ATF is among the most effective, efficient, and hard-hitting agencies in the federal government."

David A. King, chief of police of St. Charles, Missouri, was so outraged by the ad that he wrote to the International Association of Chiefs of Police to demand that the NRA, in the future, be denied the right to place an exhibit booth in the IACP's national conference exhibit hall. In fact, the association barred NRA advertising from its publication, *Police Chief Magazine*.

Dewey R. Stokes, national president of the Fraternal Order of Police, wrote to *USA Today:*

> The scariest thing about the NRA accusations is that some people believe them. The NRA must be exposed for what it is—a Washington bureaucracy bent on self-preservation at any expense, including public safety. If the NRA is successful in its effort to maul ATF, there will be no agency to trace a gun used in a crime, to stop an interstate firearms trafficker, to assure the rights of law abiding gun owners; in short to coordinate and assist in the national law enforcement effort to keep all of us safe from the illegal use of firearms. It's been said that politics is a blood sport. In the politics of gun control, if the NRA has its way, the blood may be real—and it may be ours.

In an interview, Stokes also said, "These people are out promoting violence in our profession, and every law enforcement officer in this country who does wear a badge ought to be outraged [by] what the NRA is doing."

Bob Scully, executive director of the National Association of Police Organizations, said that the cumulative effect of comments against the police from the NRA, radio talk-show hosts, and defense lawyers is deadly. "You put it all together, yes, police officers are going to lose their lives in this country."

The NRA leaders constantly circulate "statistics," claiming that a large majority of the BATF's cases are filed against law-abiding citizens. The Fraternal Order of Police calls that "recycling old lies."

Unfortunately, these are not the only lies that the NRA propaganda machine constantly circulates.

The Law Enforcement Steering Committee represents many major police organizations. On March 23, 1995, its chair, Kenneth T. Lyons, wrote a letter to President Clinton:

> This letter is sent to you by the following members of the Law Enforcement Steering Committee (LESC): the Federal Law Enforcement Officers' Association, the Fraternal Order of Police, the International Brotherhood of Police Officers, the Major Cities Chiefs Association, the National Association of Police Organizations, the National Troopers Coalition, and the Police Foundation.
>
> We urge you to join the Nation's law enforcement community in strong support of the men and women of the Bureau of Alcohol, Tobacco and Firearms. ATF

has once again come under vicious attack by the National Rifle Association, an organization devoted to turning back the progress made on firearms legislation. Recent newspaper advertisements have attacked and impugned the reputation of ATF's personnel through untruths and unfounded accusations. . . .

The NRA's attempts to criticize the enforcers of the law are without merit. In 1994, for example, 47% of the 10,000 defendants recommended by ATF for prosecution were previously convicted felons, and 49% of the 10,000 were involved in drug trafficking. Further, over the past 10 years ATF agents have executed over 10,000 search warrants. <u>None</u> of them has led to any finding of Constitutional violations by an employee acting outside the scope of authority. This is an enviable record by any standard.

This is the agency of which Wayne LaPierre wrote, in his book *Guns, Crime and Freedom,* "A February 1982 report of the Senate Judiciary Committee hearings documented that BATF has engaged almost entirely in harassing innocent citizens." Apparently, the nation's leading police organizations didn't read that report, or if they did, they wisely didn't believe it. In any event, the accusation was clearly not based on fact.

The NRA insists it is a law-and-order organization that works hand-in-glove with the police. It advertises constantly that it stands beside the police, that the nation's police and the NRA are allies in the fight against crime.

Police outrage over its ad campaign might have prompted the NRA to back down, if for no other reason than to maintain the fiction of being a friend to police officers. But the NRA was unrepentant. It did not tone down its rhetoric against the BATF, yet continued to pose as cops' best friend. The reaction of the most prominent police organizations suggests that the police don't think so. Admittedly, the NRA does have a few pet police-men it can trot out on cue to mouth its line.

The National Alliance of Stocking Gun Dealers is the largest trade organization in the firearms industry. In March 1995, its executive director, Bill Bridgewater, wrote a letter to President Clinton. Bridgewater had many things to say, but among them was this: "To reply to the NRA's absurd charges and demand for repairs or demolition of the BATF, I can only say that the BATF is **not broken now,** and thus, needs no repairs beyond those already underway." [Emphasis his]

A few days later Bridgewater wrote to Wayne LaPierre. He was considerably more blunt:

> I quite understand that since the NRA has cut so many of its shooting functions out of your budget, that your principal reason for existence has become political influence. You could try however, in the exercise of that political influence to at least not sound as though you have gone totally berserk.
>
> You absolutely must find some other way to justify your existence and your incessant appeal for more and more cash from your members without having an **enemy** to vanquish. Of late if there is no visible enemy to trash, then you must invent one. You look damned foolish when you do, and you often do damage you don't realize.
>
> In summary, your ad is as far from a "patriotic drive" as it is possible to get. In addition, you do more

damage to the industry with this vitriolic garbage than you can understand and appreciate.

In the meantime, <u>you don't represent the firearms industry! Leave the regulation of the industry to the industry and its regulators</u>. [Emphasis his, throughout]

In May 1995, three sporting-goods expositions in Texas banned NRA recruiting booths. Jerry Curl, show director of the Texas-Mexico Hunting and Fishing Expos, said he had talked to other exhibitors and sportsmen all over Texas and that there was all but unanimous agreement that the NRA was "heading in the wrong direction."

Bob Lockett, president of a shooting-sports business called the Second Amendment, wrote to his representative in Congress:

> The National Rifle Association is a consumer oriented, fund raising organization based in Falls Church, Virginia. <u>The NRA does not speak for me. The NRA does not speak for my shooting sports business. The NRA does not speak for the firearms and shooting sports industry.</u> The NRA speaks only for the self aggrandizing leadership of the NRA in the name of soliciting more money from the membership.

In a letter to the BATF, Robert W. Gates, national sales manager for Glock, Inc., manufacturer of those pistols with the plastic parts, disassociated his company from the "inflammatory" advertising of the NRA.

Richard J. Feldman, executive director of the American Shooting Sports Council, called BATF agents "extremely professional" and characterized the NRA ads as "totally inappropriate."

Congressman Jim Lightfoot, a Republican from Iowa, issued a statement:

> I am a member of the NRA. I have been for years and am honored to have their election support. [The NRA gave him $9,900 for his 1994 campaign.] If you check my voting record, you'll see I am a staunch supporter of Second Amendment rights. . . . But I honestly do not understand why NRA is determined to portray ATF in a misleading light. The NRA's ad does not fit the established facts. The ATF is neither out of control nor do I believe it violates the Bill of Rights. . . . In my view, NRA is shooting at the wrong target. ATF only enforces the laws passed by Congress.

Finally, Joanne Heckman, a citizen with no particular industry or political affiliation, wrote a letter to President Clinton, saying, "Whatever you're doing to annoy the NRA, please do more of it."

LaPierre and his colleagues were not at all ruffled by the angry reaction to their "Tell the Clinton White House to Stay Out of Your House" ad or the "jack-booted thugs" letter. The letter, which achieved a new low in vicious invectives, deserves to be quoted at some length. All the boldface and underlining in the following text was in the original letter.

> **Fact #1. The Congress' leading anti-gunners, Senators Diane [sic] Feinstein, Ted Kennedy and Congressmen Charles Schumer and Major Owens all survived their last elections.**
>
> They've pledged to fight to the bitter end for Brady II and its ammo taxes, licensing and registration schemes, gun rationing, bureaucrats with the power to

determine if you "need" a gun and yes, the repeal of the Second Amendment.

It doesn't matter to them that the Brady Law is a failure.

It doesn't matter to them that the Brady Law has become one more tool that government agents are using to deny the Constitutional rights of law-abiding citizens.

It doesn't matter to them that the semi-auto [the NRA term for assault rifle] ban gives jack-booted thugs more power to take away our Constitutional rights, break in our doors, seize our guns, destroy our property, and even injure or kill us. . . .

Fact #3. President Clinton's army of anti-gun government agents continues to intimidate and harass law-abiding citizens.

In Clinton's administration, if you have a badge you have the government's go-ahead to harass, intimidate, even to murder law-abiding citizens.

Randy Weaver at Ruby Ridge . . . Waco and the Branch Davidians . . . Not too long ago it was unthinkable for Federal agents wearing Nazi bucket helmets and black storm trooper uniforms to attack law-abiding citizens

Not today. Not with Clinton. . . .

Most Americans don't realize that our freedoms are slowly slipping away.

They don't understand that politicians and bureaucrats are chipping away at the American way of life.

They're <u>destroying</u> business, <u>destroying</u> our economy, <u>destroying</u> property rights, <u>destroying</u> our moral foundation, <u>destroying</u> our schools, <u>destroying</u> our culture . . .

. . . <u>Destroying</u> our Constitution.

And the attack, either through legislation or

regulation, on the Second Amendment is only the first in a long campaign to destroy the freedoms at the core of our American life.

You can see it in the gun bans, certainly. But you can also see it in closed ranges, closed hunting lands, confiscated collectors' firearms, banned magazines, and ammunition taxes.

You can see it when jack-booted government thugs, wearing black, armed to the teeth, break down a door, open fire with an automatic weapon, and kill or maim law-abiding citizens.

America's gun owners will only be the first to lose their freedoms.

<u>If we lose the right to keep and bear arms, then the right to free speech, free practice of religion, and every other freedom in the Bill of Rights are sure to follow.</u>

Since the letter went only to members of the NRA, it did not draw much fire at first. After the Oklahoma City bombing, a new firestorm of criticism was directed at the NRA and at LaPierre personally. Senator Bob Kerrey, a wounded veteran of the Vietnam War and Vietnam recipient of the Congressional Medal of Honor, spoke to the National Press Club, warning: "Political appeals to white male gun owners as victims of government oppression can unintentionally provide a silent refuge to right-wing extremists who believe violence is a reasonable means."

Vic O'Boyski, president of the Federal Law Enforcement Officers Association, accused the NRA leadership of "demonizing dedicated men and women who are going after criminals." He went on to charge that the NRA was "feeding delusionary conspiracy theories."

Josh Sugarman, executive director of the Violence Policy Center, said, "The NRA has validated the paranoia out there about imminent confiscation of guns."

Carefully researched articles in the *Washington Post* and the *Los Angeles Times,* among others, totally repudiated LaPierre's claims against the BATF. Yet LaPierre did not back down. Appearing on *Meet the Press,* he said, "Those words are not far—in fact they are a pretty close description of what's happening in the real world."

The most noted criticism of the LaPierre letter came from former president George Bush. A few years earlier, the NRA had grandly awarded him a life membership. Now he had resigned. His letter to Thomas L. Washington, president of the National Rifle Association, is worth quoting at length:

> I was outraged when, even in the wake of the Oklahoma City tragedy, Mr. Wayne LaPierre, Executive Vice President of NRA, defended his attack on federal agents as "jack-booted thugs." To attack Secret Service agents or ATF people or any government law enforcement people as "wearing Nazi bucket helmets and black storm trooper uniforms" wanting to attack law-abiding citizens is a vicious slander on good people. . . .
>
> I am a gun owner and an avid hunter. Over the years I have agreed with most of NRA's objectives, particularly your educational and training efforts, and your fundamental stance in favor of owning guns.
>
> However, your broadside against Federal agents deeply offends my own sense of decency and honor, and it offends my concept of service to country. It indirectly slanders a wide array of government law

enforcement officials, who are out there, day and night, laying their lives on the line for all of us.

You have not repudiated Mr. LaPierre's unwarranted attack. Therefore, I resign as a Life Member of NRA, said resignation to be effective upon your receipt of this letter. Please remove my name from your membership list.

Still, the NRA did not back down. In mid-May it ran a big ad containing an open letter to former president Bush. Based on its own versions of events in Waco and elsewhere, the NRA offered no apology for the "jack-booted thugs" letter and insisted that Americans are in danger of losing all their freedoms.

NRA board member Neal Knox responded petulantly: "George Bush has been feuding with the NRA since 1992, when we decided we couldn't back him. He's been biding his time since then, waiting for the right time to kick us in the shins."

The NRA had endorsed Bush in 1988 but would not do so in 1992 because he had banned the importation of certain assault weapons. This had so inflamed Second Amendment fundamentalists that at the 1991 NRA convention some members wanted to expel then-President Bush from the organization. An effort to do so was actually made but was beaten back by the leadership.

President Bush's resignation had apparently made no impression. Nor had the earlier resignations of General Norman Schwarzkopf and Colorado senator Ben Nighthorse Campbell. Nor had the resignation from the NRA board of directors of Michigan congressman John D. Dingell, a staunch opponent of gun control. Dingell had himself referred to some BATF agents as "jack-booted American fascists" and believed the BATF was an agency out of control. He wanted to vote for the crime bill, to put more police on the streets to combat crime in America. The bill contained the assault-rifle ban. Though he opposed the assault-rifle ban, he believed the overall bill was good for America. He resigned from the NRA and voted for the bill.

After the "jack-booted thugs" letter was distributed, Dingell wrote to Tom Washington and Wayne LaPierre:

> I have, as you know, sharply criticized the actions of the Bureau of Alcohol, Tobacco and Firearms. . . . However (and this is a substantial however): the language and rhetoric used in your fundraising appeal go far beyond any of my comments in their generality, and in the ludicrous and offensive implication that federal agents are encouraged to commit acts of violence against ordinary citizens. . . .
>
> I am greatly concerned that the letter's language, and this debate, endangers the future effectiveness of efforts to protect our Second Amendment rights, and particularly damages the NRA. In the wake of the Oklahoma City bombing, we would all be well-advised to choose our words on these matters more carefully and to promote the return in America to civil discourse on public issues.

Senator Bob Dole delicately handled the issue from the Republican side, saying in a televised statement that the NRA needed "a little image adjustment here." The only Republican senators to denounce the "jack-booted thugs" letter were Alan Simpson of Wyoming and Olympia Snowe of Maine. Simpson said he would meet with Thomas Washington and ask him to repudiate "that exaggerated, pathetic, almost totally inflammatory letter."

Snowe said she was "very disappointed" with the inflammatory language that the NRA used, and believes the NRA should apologize.

A month after the letter went out, LaPierre did apologize for it, in an oblique way. He said, "I feel really bad about the fact that the words in that letter have been interpreted to apply to all federal law enforcement officers. If anyone thought the intention was to paint all federal law enforcement officers with the same brush, I'm sorry, and I apologize."

Good for him. But his apology sounds as if he hadn't read his own letter.

NRA members at their annual convention in Phoenix groused about the apology, saying LaPierre should have stood by his statements. NRA insiders say that's how Neal Knox and Tanya Metaksa feel. The apology, not the letter, briefly put LaPierre's job in jeopardy.

There is no end to the NRA's intransigence. After the Oklahoma City bombing, some lawmakers revived an idea that had been on the back burner: tag explosives with microscopic chemical chips, called "taggants," so they can be traced. In the debris of a violent explosion, these markers will often, though not always, enable investigators to determine where the explosives were manufactured and maybe even pinpoint a distributor.

Also, fertilizers can be treated with defuser chemicals that make fertilizers much more difficult to detonate. In other nations, ammonium-nitrate fertilizers must be mixed with ground limestone, which makes a better fertilizer as well as making the ammonium nitrate less practical to use as an explosive. Representative W. J. Tauzin of Louisiana hopes fertilizer manufacturers will voluntarily add defusers to their products, but he is prepared to introduce legislation to require it if they don't.

What could be more reasonable? What could be less harmful to any legitimate interest? Who could argue against it?

The NRA could. The gun lobby and explosives makers have repeatedly fought to defeat bills that would have required taggants in explosives and defusers in fertilizers. Taggants, say the NRA, could interfere with the stability of cartridges and shotgun shells made by hobbyists who hand-load ammunition.

Does that outweigh the help to investigators tracking terrorist bombers or the impact a tracer might have in discouraging bombers? How many people make a hobby of hand-loading ammunition? Is their interest superior to the interests of the victims crushed in the explosions at the World Trade Center in New York and the Alfred P. Murrah Federal Building in Oklahoma City?

Where is the public interest here?

The public interest may have little to do with the NRA's policy. Several members of the NRA board of directors are manufacturers of gunpowder and/or reloading equipment. What is more, gunpowder makers and manufacturers of hand-loading equipment buy a lot of advertising space in *American Rifleman,* the NRA magazine.

Why the hysterical attacks on BATF? Bill Bridgewater explained it best in his letter, quoted earlier: "You absolutely must find some other way to justify your existence and your incessant appeal for more and more cash from your members without having an **enemy** to vanquish. Of late if there is no visible enemy to trash, then you must invent one."

Unhappily, some people believe the BATF is the villain. Some members of Congress profess to believe it. Some members of Congress want to abolish the BATF altogether. Through one side of their mouths they tout law and order. But because of NRA animosity toward the BATF, they want to weaken one of the most effective law enforcement agencies of the federal government.

Stranger yet, under prompting from the NRA, some in Congress have taken to vilifying the FBI and the U.S. Marshals Service as well.

Even stranger, it is the Clinton administration and Democrats in Congress that are defending the law enforcement agencies against these NRA-inspired attacks. The two parties have done a complete role reversal. In 1995 it was the Democrats who were for anti-crime legislation, anti-terrorism legislation, and so on; but because the NRA abhors some minor new gun-control recommendations in these bills, they push congressional Republicans into opposition.

Guns have made for strange bedfellows.

CHAPTER SEVEN
WACO AND RUBY RIDGE

The National Rifle Association has made martyrs out of two odd characters, not because either is particularly heroic, but because both came in the crosshairs of the Bureau of Alcohol, Tobacco and Firearms.

Randy Weaver is a Vietnam veteran and a Green Beret. For ten years he and his family lived in Idaho, in a plywood shack on a mountainside called Ruby Ridge, four miles from the nearest paved road. The Weavers did not send their children to school, preferring to teach them at home so strangers would not sully the children's minds. The family scratched out a living by hunting, growing a garden, and canning food in Mason jars. They also accumulated a considerable stock of weapons.

Randy Weaver was and is an avowed white separatist. He may have been a member of or may have just had friends in the Aryan Nation, a white-supremacist hate group headquartered in northern Idaho. He entertained radical political notions, such as the idea that the federal government had no jurisdiction over him.

In October 1989, Weaver sold two sawed-off shotguns in

violation of the National Firearms Act of 1934. Unfortunately for him, the buyer sprang a little surprise. The man, who Weaver thought was a friend, was an informant for Weaver's nemesis, the BATF. In January 1991, BATF agents arrested Weaver. He was released on his own recognizance under an order to appear in court at a later date.

When that day arrived, he did not appear in court. More than that, in letters and messages delivered through friends, Weaver and his wife, Vicki, threatened to shoot anyone who came to arrest him. The Weavers were armed and dangerous. Vicki Weaver had once written a letter to an attorney, warning that "the tyrant's blood would flow." Allegedly, they had also sent threatening letters to then-president Reagan.

Since Weaver had not appeared in court and refused to do so, the BATF passed the case to the U.S. Marshals Service. Marshals, surveying the situation, were convinced the Weavers meant what they said and would shoot anyone who approached them to serve the arrest warrant. The marshals mounted a major operation to serve the warrant on Randy Weaver. In effect, they mounted a siege, which continued for months.

In August 1992, the marshals closed in on Ruby Ridge. What followed is not entirely clear. There has been conflicting testimony. What is certain is that in the hail of gunfire that followed, Weaver's son, Sammy, his wife, Vicki, and William Degan, a deputy U.S. marshal, were all shot and killed. Fourteen-year-old Sammy fell in the first day of the siege in a gunfight that began when one of the marshals shot Sammy's dog.

Weaver's friend, Kevin Harris, was in the shack. He was an adult and a sharpshooter. Two marshals testified that Harris fired the shot that killed Degan. Although both Weaver and Harris were acquitted of murder, Kevin Harris subsequently testified before a Senate subcommittee that he probably did kill Degan.

With one marshal killed, an FBI SWAT team moved in on the second day of the siege. The orders given FBI sharpshooters are not entirely clear either. They shot and killed Vicki Weaver as she stood in the doorway of the cabin, her baby in her arms. She was apparently holding the cabin door open so that Randy Weaver could run for cover from the gunfire of the federal snipers.

In the summer of 1995 congressional hearings were held on the Ruby Ridge shootout. Randy Weaver testified that he would have surrendered to a county sheriff if one had come to serve the warrant, which, he charged, the sheriff lacked the courage to do. He testified that one of the marshals wounded Sammy in the arm and then shot him in the back as the boy attempted to run back into the cabin.

No one denied that Sammy fired back at the marshals, maybe because he had seen the marshals shoot his dog. The marshals testified that it was Weaver himself who accidentally shot Sammy in the back. Their evidence was that Sammy was killed with a 9mm round. Only Weaver himself, and one marshal who couldn't have fired the shot, had 9mm weapons.

As to the death of Vicki Weaver, that remains a mystery too. The sharpshooter who killed her was firing at Kevin Harris. It has been suggested that he hit her accidentally, maybe because she moved at the instant the shot was fired.

Weaver was acquitted of murder. No one could prove he had fired the shot that killed the deputy marshal. He was also acquitted on the charge of selling sawed-off shotguns, on the basis that the BATF had entrapped him.

There is no question that the entire operation was botched. Neither the BATF nor the FBI did itself any favors in the violent way the arrest was carried out, or in the aftermath when investigations were mishandled. There is strong evidence that the federal agencies worked harder at covering their own backsides than at uncovering the truth.

But exactly how a lawful arrest warrant could have been served on Randy Weaver without a violent confrontation, no one seems to know. He had said he would fire on anyone who came to serve the warrant, and he did. He defied the law. He defied the government of the United States. Whatever faults anyone can find in the way the marshals and the FBI agents conducted themselves, one fact is inescapable: that Randy Weaver, like others of his ilk, was expecting Armageddon and, by his own intransigence, brought it about. His arrogant, egomaniacal refusal to acknowledge the simple fact that every citizen is subject to the law is the ultimate cause of the showdown on Ruby Ridge.

In Randy Weaver, the NRA has found a hero, if for no reason other than that the villain in the case was the "jack-booted" BATF. The truth is that the BATF identified the man on whom the warrant was to be served, then stood aside. The U.S. Marshals Service attempted to serve the warrant. When a marshal was killed, the FBI moved in with sharpshooters.

Someone in the Weaver cabin killed the marshal. Maybe Sammy Weaver was killed by a marshal after the boy had fired on the marshals, or maybe Sammy was accidentally shot by his father—a horrible thing for Randy Weaver to contemplate. Vicki

Weaver was accidentally shot by an FBI sharpshooter who was shooting at Harris. No one from the BATF fired a shot. But that hasn't stopped the NRA from placing the blame there.

The NRA's second martyr is David Koresh, a self-appointed prophet-potentate of the Branch Davidian sect in Waco, Texas. This NRA hero is eerily reminiscent of Jim Jones, who led more than 900 of his followers to their deaths in Guyana in 1979. Koresh was an arrogant, dictatorial, sadistic child molester who assembled the most addle-brained of his few followers in a compound near Waco. There he hypnotized them with apocalyptic twaddle and urged them to prepare for suicide.

The compound was a rambling wooden building, erected with total disregard of fire laws. The residents called it Mt. Carmel, a reverent and pastoral name for what was actually a sprawling firetrap. The cultists who assembled in it armed themselves with semiautomatic rifles, including a .50-caliber rifle, and hand grenades. It was those weapons that put the compound on the BATF radar screen. An alert United Parcel Service driver reported to a local deputy sheriff that the Davidians were receiving deliveries of grenade casings and explosives.

The Davidians expected the government would come along eventually and interrupt their twisted existence, and they were determined to resist with firepower. Interference, sooner or later, was bound to come. The compound was an arsenal, where the Davidians allegedly were converting semiautomatic weapons into fully automatic weapons, in violation of federal law. Witnesses testified that Koresh was looking for a fight with federal authorities. While he waited for Armageddon, Koresh passed the time preaching, prophesying doom, and having sex with underage girls, some of whom he called his wives. He required celibacy of many of the male cultists and ordered them to give their wives to him.

The Justice Department had heard reports of child abuse at the compound, but the full extent of Koresh's perversion was not known until after his death when Congress held hearings on the final battle at Mt. Carmel. Over the opposition of some Republicans, who did not want her testimony to be heard, Kiri Jewell, fourteen, testified before the congressional hearing that Koresh sexually abused her in a Texas motel when she was only ten years old. Here is part of Kiri Jewell's indictment against the "martyr" David Koresh:

> David was very strict about how we should live. He only spanked me twice, though I knew he spanked other people or had them spanked. He personally spanked me because I said I was going on a diet when I was about eight years old. He used the big wooden board they used for adults, not the wooden spoon they called "little helper."
>
> It was common for David to sleep in a bed with women and children. . . . I didn't even think about it, because the women and girls were all David's wives, or would be, and many of the kids were his too. Even if he wasn't really our father, we were taught that he was our real father. . . .
>
> We all knew about sex, because David talked about it a lot. He made us watch movies that showed sex and war. . . .
>
> My mom and Lisa went to do a little shopping. I took a shower, and then I was brushing my hair, sitting in a chair, and David told me to come and sit down by

him in the bed. I was wearing a long white T-shirt and panties. He kissed me and sat there. But then he laid me down. [Here Kiri describes, in painful detail, kissing and genital fondling of her by Koresh.] I had known this would happen sometime, so I just laid there and stared at the ceiling. I didn't know how to kiss him back. Anyway, I was still kind of freaked out.

When he was finished he told me to go take a shower. . . . I just stayed in the shower for maybe an hour. When I came out David was in his jeans and the bed was made. He told me to come here again. This time he read to me from the Song of Solomon. I was ten years old when this happened.

In many states what Kiri described is defined in the criminal codes as "gross sexual imposition" and when performed against a minor is punished by a long term, or even life, in prison.

Kiri testified that Koresh spanked children with boat oars, that he "married" a fourteen-year-old girl and impregnated her. She also testified that Koresh instructed the children on how best to commit suicide: by shoving the muzzle of a pistol into the soft spot at the back of the mouth and then pulling the trigger.

Kiri Jewell was fortunate enough to have left the Branch Davidian compound before the BATF raid. Thus, she was not there during the siege and was not burned to death at the behest of her "father," David Koresh.

On February 28, 1993, agents of the BATF came to the Branch Davidian compound with a warrant that authorized them to search for illegal weapons. They had ample evidence not only that several hundred firearms were stored in the compound, but that some of them were semiautomatic weapons converted to automatic fire. Given that intelligence, the agents did not knock on the door but attempted to break in. The wisdom of that decision will be debated long after Koresh's sins are forgotten.

One law enforcement officer, who is not of the BATF, has said the day has passed when marshals or sheriffs or any other officers can arrive in three-piece suits, politely knock on doors, and hand a warrant to the person who opens the door. In serious cases, more often than not, warrants are served by breaking in. Too many times there is deadly firepower inside.

That is what happened at Waco. The cultists opened fire. There is no question that the Davidians fired first. If we don't trust federal reports on that subject, we can accept the word of the Texas Rangers who witnessed the event and who unanimously say the cultists fired first. Four agents were killed in the gunfire, as were six Davidians.

A fifty-one-day siege followed, a siege that was frequently televised and heavily covered. Americans sat as a jury rendering simultaneous judgment on the events as they unfolded. The television coverage gave the NRA something it didn't get out of the Ruby Ridge fight—a front-row view of the "jack-booted thugs" as they surrounded a small religious cult and moved in for Armageddon.

The fifty-one days passed agonizingly, with federal agents trying to persuade Koresh to surrender. He befuddled the issue, playing for time by reciting biblical texts. Robert Rodriguez, an undercover Treasury agent, spoke to Koresh on the morning of April 19, 1993. Koresh told Rodriguez, "Robert, neither the ATF nor the National Guard will ever get me."

Later that day the FBI lobbed tear gas into the compound and moved in with tanks that smashed through the walls. But it was the Davidians themselves who set Mt. Carmel on fire. The evidence I have seen leaves me with no doubt that accelerants had been strategically placed throughout the flimsy building. Within less than a minute the structure was engulfed in roaring flames, just as Koresh, in his suicidal fantasies, knew it would be.

More than eighty Branch Davidians died in the fire, including twenty-two children. David Koresh was one of the dead.

His message had been so thoroughly pounded into his followers that they willingly followed him to his maker and dragged their screaming children with them. FBI agent James McGee risked his life, entering the flaming building in an attempt to rescue a woman. She fought him off. When he asked her where the children were, she refused to tell him. She died in the fire, and so did the children.

Was the assault on the compound mishandled? Koresh could have been arrested on one of his frequent trips to town before the standoff began. But that would not have freed the BATF agents from their duty to go into the compound and investigate the allegations of weapons stockpiling. The agents who stormed the compound were not there to arrest Koresh but to locate a cache of illegal weapons. They had been informed that Koresh knew they were coming. Should they have postponed the raid? Would Koresh have surrendered in a few more days had the FBI waited him out? Would he have spent those few more days sexually preying on children and twisting the minds of his followers with gibberish?

I don't have the answers to those questions, and neither does the NRA nor the BATF agents who made the decisions and must live with the tragic outcome. But it doesn't take the wisdom of hindsight to conclude that David Koresh was no martyr. He was a dangerous man with a gang of foolish disciples. And, like Randy Weaver, Koresh irrationally believed he was not subject to the laws that govern every other citizen and felt he could make his own rules.

Napoleon Bonaparte once said, "I am not an ordinary man, and the rules that govern ordinary men do not apply to me." David Koresh might have done Napoleon one better when he said, "I am God's chosen instrument, and the laws that govern mere mortals do not apply to me."

The inescapable truth is that ultimate responsibility for the tragedy of Waco lies directly on David Koresh. He was not attacked by "jack-booted thugs," and he is no martyr. He was nothing but a common felon—worse, a perverted molester trying to evade responsibility for his crimes. And it is he who is responsible for the deaths of more than eighty people.

It is the duty of law officers to serve warrants, subpoenas, and other judicial processes. It is the duty of law-abiding citizens to accept them and abide by them. If they are improper, the courts will determine so. That is where disputes about the propriety of warrants and other legal processes must be decided: in courts of law, not by armed resistance. Apart from the innocent children who died in the fire, Koresh and his followers bear sole responsibility for their own fate. If they had accepted a lawful service of process like any other citizen, the entire tragic Waco episode would not have happened.

It verges on insanity to say that the Davidians were defending themselves. Defending against what? If a police officer tries to stop me for a traffic violation, am I entitled to defend myself by shooting him? Suppose a police officer comes to my home in the middle of the night to arrest me for murder, and he is wrong; he has come to the wrong house. Am I entitled to defend myself by killing him? I am not. I am obliged to submit to arrest and then to demonstrate his error, probably at the police station, and if not there, then in a court of law.

What kind of society, what kind of nation, would we have if every person imagined he or she had a right to "defend" himself or herself with deadly force against a law officer acting rightly or wrongfully? We would have the kind of society that exists only in the paranoid imaginings of the NRA leadership.

During the summer of 1995, the Oversight Subcommittee on Criminal Justice, a subcommittee of the House Government Reform and Oversight Committee, held hearings on Ruby Ridge and Waco. It was a political dog-and-pony show the likes of which I have seen too often in Washington.

The subcommittee cochairmen were Representative Bill Zeliff, a Republican from New Hampshire, and Representative Bill McCollum, a Republican from Florida.

For political reasons, Republicans in Congress have struggled to put their own spin on the Waco tragedy. In this they have had willing assistance from the NRA. In fact, NRA participation in scripting the hearings was so egregious that there is some justification behind the Democrats' charges that the hearings were not held to determine what happened—what mistakes were made and how to avoid similar events in future—but were held simply to help the NRA trash the BATF.

The credibility of the hearings was hopelessly compromised when it became known that NRA employees had been deeply involved in gathering information for the committee. In fact, the NRA funded some of the congressional "investigation." Chairman Zeliff, who accused President Clinton of a Waco cover-up, dodged and squirmed to prevent public disclosure of the NRA involvement in what was supposed to be a congressional inquiry.

But I am convinced by the evidence I have had access to that the NRA and its lapdogs in Congress worked hand-in-paw to skew those important hearings. At least one NRA employee contacted witnesses and represented herself as a member of the House committee staff. Joyce Sparks, a Texas social worker who had visited the Davidian compound to look into the conditions for the children, brought to the committee an answering-machine tape on which a caller named Fran Haga was recorded as saying she was with the team that was putting together the Waco hearings. Dr. Alan Stone, another witness, testified that Haga also contacted him and represented herself as a member of the committee staff.

The NRA had an explanation. Tanya Metaksa said that the NRA had formed a team to investigate Waco and that it was this team Haga was talking about, without intent to deceive.

It doesn't wash. Here is an excerpt from the transcript of the Waco hearings. It begins with the playing of the answering-machine tape.

FEMALE VOICE: I'm at 202-543-6000, extension 102. That's in Washington, D.C. And I expect that this is not exactly the voice that you want to hear on your voice mail this morning, but I'm with the Waco hearing team that is working on putting together the Waco hearings. . . . And I was trying to get in touch with you to chat with you about some of your direct knowledge of the things that came down in Waco. If you can get back to me, please do.

REP. [CHARLES] SCHUMER: Did you return Fran Haga's call?

MS. SPARKS: Yes, I did.

REP. SCHUMER: When you called her back, how did she initially identify herself?

MS. SPARKS: She said she was with the Waco team and she wanted to talk to me about what I knew about Waco.

REP. SCHUMER: Okay. And how did you get her to admit she worked for the NRA?

MS. SPARKS: As we talked, something just didn't seem right, and I asked her, "What is your role? Tell me about your role in this." Because it seemed to be getting fuzzy to me. She sort of talked around in circles. And finally I said, "Wait a minute. Who pays your salary?" And when pressed, she did tell me that it was the National Rifle Association.

REP. SCHUMER: Did you feel deceived by Ms. Haga?

MS. SPARKS: Yes.

A minute later the chairman of the subcommittee, Representative Bill Zeliff, interjected:

REP. ZELIFF: May I ask, what was the point? Did I miss something?

REP. SCHUMER: Yeah, what you missed—well, I don't think anybody in the audience missed it, Mr. Chairman. (Laughter.)

Representative Henry Hyde, Republican of Illinois and Chairman of the House Judiciary Committee, wrote a letter to Representative Charles E. Schumer, Democrat, New York, saying, "I share your outrage over an apparent attempt by an outside party to mislead a Texas social worker. No such contact was ever authorized by myself or this committee."

I have learned that witnesses scheduled to go before the committee were interviewed by NRA staff members before they testified. One witness received money from a legal defense fund established by the NRA. At the hearings, an NRA staff attorney sat in a section reserved for House staff until someone identified her.

In June 1995, congressional staffers arrived in Texas to look into certain aspects of the Waco tragedy. Among the experts traveling with the congressional staff were representatives of a firm called Failure Analysis Associates, who proposed to x-ray the remnants of forty-eight guns found in the ashes of the compound to see if they had in fact been converted from semiautomatic to full-automatic weapons. Not a bad idea, except that I discovered these experts didn't work for Congress but for the NRA. When these experts were exposed as NRA plants, the Justice Department refused to allow them to examine the guns.

Chairman Zeliff insisted that the arrangement was approved by the House Ethics Committee—conveniently overlooking the fact that the Ethics Committee was never told the NRA would be paying the experts.

The Republicans on the committee had their own agenda and did not want to be distracted. "These hearings are not just about the NRA and fourteen-year-old girls," groused Committee Cochair Zeliff. Freshman Republican Representative Frederick

W. Heineman of North Carolina discounted Kiri Jewell's testimony, saying, "We know that Koresh was a pervert. We're not here to make a point of that."

Neal Knox wrote in his column, "The Neal Knox Report," that "child sexual abuse is immaterial—that's sure not BATF's jurisdiction."

According to reports filed with the Federal Election Commission as required by law, Representative Zeliff received from the NRA Political Victory Fund a contribution of $10,900 for his 1994 re-election campaign fund. For 1992 he received $9,900. For his 1990 campaign he received $4,000.

The *Wall Street Journal* is not known generally as a left-wing, liberal publication. In its July 13, 1995, issue, it ran an article by Albert R. Hunt that sums up this case against Congress:

> A driving force behind these hearings is a payoff to the politically powerful National Rifle Association. The NRA has listed the need for Congress "to investigate the abuse by federal agents" as one of its top priorities. Surreptitiously, the NRA's lobbyists have been prowling around Capitol Hill briefing selective staffers and members on Waco and plotting strategy for the coming hearings. . . .
>
> Whatever the justification for hearings, it's inarguably true that the paranoia about Waco is linked to the Oklahoma City bombing and these congressional hearings run the risk of appearing to be a response to that tragedy. There's a simple way to avoid that: also hold hearings on the growing right-wing, gun-crazed militia movement. Far more Americans, polls show, see

a clear and present danger in these militia movements than in federal law enforcement officers.

The article cited a *Wall Street Journal*/NBC News poll that showed only 21 percent of Americans thought it was important to hold hearings on Waco, while 62 percent thought it was important to hold them on the private militia groups.

A *Sacramento Bee* editorial agreed with the need for a hearing on the militias:

> So why not at least follow a congressional trashing of law enforcers with a hearing investigating potential lawbreakers, especially since militias are widely reported to be growing since the [Oklahoma City] bombing? . . .
>
> The irrational answer is obvious: The gun counterculture and its NRA patrons vote Republican. This is also why the speaker created a gun task force including such representatives as Helen Chenoweth and Steve Stockman, both of whom have echoed the militias and the extreme gun lobby in demonizing law enforcement agencies.
>
> Putting this pair on a gun task force is the 1995 equivalent of, say, President George McGovern appointing Stokely Carmichael and Abbie Hoffman to top jobs at the FBI.

Carl Rowan, national syndicated columnist for the *Chicago Sun-Times*, wrote:

> You surely ask why some House members are looking for political gain in the tragic ashes of that 1993 siege of the Branch Davidian compound in Waco, Texas. . . .

You surely know that the National Rifle Association is pushing this hearing out of some abysmal notion that if federal officials can raid the Davidians because they stockpiled machine guns, hand grenades and other terrible weapons to use against law enforcement officials, then federal agents will soon raid homes where "ordinary citizens" keep AK-47s and other automatic weapons that are banned in this country. . . .

What fair-minded person can fail to be overwhelmed by Wednesday's chilling testimony of 14-year-old Kiri Jewell about how the Davidians' leader, David Koresh, introduced her to sex when she was 10? Who thinks Koresh had some religious shield against statutory rape laws that allowed him to "marry" and produce a baby by a 14-year-old friend of Kiri's?

I am inclined to believe the FBI carried out a cover-up of its mistakes.

But I find baseless and offensive the assertion by Rep. Bill McCollum (R-Fla.), chairman of the House Judiciary Committee Subcommittee on Crime, that "all of these deaths were the result of federal government action." What blame does McCollum impute to Koresh and his actions?

In an article he wrote for *Guns & Ammo* magazine, Congressman Steve Stockman said the Branch Davidians "were burned to death because they had guns that the government did not wish them to have." He also said that the White House meant the Waco raid "to be a lesson to gun owners all over America: Don't own firearms that the government does not like." Stockman, who got generous support from the NRA in the 1994 election campaign, also wrote that the federal government "executed" the Branch Davidians.

Investigation of the militias is not likely to happen in this Congress.

CHAPTER EIGHT

HANDGUNS: KILLERS OR PROTECTORS?

Bernard Goetz was sitting quietly in his seat on a subway when a group of young men approached him. They asked him for money. He believed he was being threatened. He pulled a pistol and fired. To many people he was, and is, a hero.

After a hurricane hit southern Florida, people put up signs on the wreckage of their homes and businesses that read: YOU LOOT, WE SHOOT! Many applauded.

During the Los Angeles riots following the first trial of the police officers accused in the Rodney King beating, some owners of small businesses sat on their roofs armed with rifles, ready to fire on looters.

Hardly a week goes by in New York City when some shopkeeper is not proclaimed a hero for shooting at a robber.

To a large number of frightened people, these are satisfying justifiable scenarios.

But are they realistic, or are they fantasies?

Congressional hearings have featured testimony by many witnesses who told stories about how having a gun available had saved their lives and/or the lives of others. Most of the stories were very appealing. The difficulty with such testimony is that it is anecdotal evidence, consisting of selected stories chosen to reinforce a point of view. Equally appealing stories, and many more of them, can be told about people who were killed or seriously wounded when they pulled guns and tried to defend themselves.

And there are countless stories about people who bought guns to protect themselves and their homes and wound up killing themselves or others in their homes because they did not know how to handle a gun. The NRA teaches courses in gun safety but opposes any law that would make such training mandatory before obtaining a license to buy a gun.

Anecdotal evidence is not statistical. Statistics that are available suggest that 45 percent of all people who try to defend themselves with guns become gun victims instead. A study published in the *New England Journal of Medicine* indicates that in cases of forced entry into a home, the risk of violence to gun owners was slightly greater than the risk to those who had no guns.

A study of 200 home invasions in Atlanta showed that only three of those victims used firearms for protection, and one of them was robbed anyway. Those who screamed or called 911 achieved about the same measure of protection. This study was published in the *Journal of the American Medical Association* and focused on violence as a public health problem. Its chief author, Dr. Arthur L. Kellerman of Emory University, said the study suggests that "the protective benefit of keeping a gun in the home has been oversold."

New York City Police Commissioner Raymond Kelly said, "There is nothing to indicate you're safer with a gun in your home." Most gun owners never even manage to reach their guns in time when a burglar does break in.

Worse, hardly a week goes by without a news story of a child shot, hurt, and often killed by a gun kept in the home in the honest belief that it is there for protection. Here is a sampling:

➤ *Mississippi.* A toddler goes into the family living room to admire the lights on the Christmas tree. In his excitement he jumps up and down, which triggers a motion detector. His mother, hearing the alarm, grabs her .38-caliber semiautomatic, runs for the living room, and fires at the first thing she sees moving. She kills her son.

➤ *Texas.* A two-year-old boy shoots himself in the leg with a handgun kept by his mother for her protection and his. Ordinarily, she kept it out of his reach but left it on the floor by her bed after she thought she heard a prowler. The boy found it, began playing with it, and shot himself.

➤ *California.* An eleven-year-old boy finds a pistol under his parents' bed. He shows it to his two-year-old stepsister and tells her, "Don't ever play with this." The pistol goes off, and the slug hits her in the head.

➤ *Louisiana.* A girl hiding in a closet jumps out and yells, "Boo!" at her father as he returns home late one night. Startled, he pulls out the concealed .357 Magnum he is carrying and shoots her dead.

➤ *New York.* The four-year-old son of two police detectives shoots himself in the head with his mother's service revolver.

➤ *Ohio.* Two brothers, ages thirteen and fourteen, are playing with a .22-caliber rifle, thinking it is not loaded. The thirteen-year-old shoots his brother in the back of the head.

➤ *New York.* A woman finds a handgun in the trash and puts it in a desk drawer. Her seven-year-old son finds it, plays with it, and shoots his five-year-old brother in the head.

➤ *Georgia.* A three-year-old boy sees an interesting object sticking out from under his mother's mattress. He reaches in to pull it out. He grabs it by the trigger and shoots himself in the face. His mother had the gun to protect the home from intruders.

➤ *Connecticut.* A boy, age twelve, accidentally shoots his friend, also twelve, in the back of the head with a .22-caliber pistol.

➤ *Ohio.* Two boys are in a bathroom. One is showing the other his father's pistol. It goes off. One boy dies.

Anecdotal evidence? Sure. But the advocates of reasonable gun control can match the NRA, story for story, against the parade of witnesses hauled into Washington to testify about how their lives were saved by their guns.

The Center to Prevent Handgun Violence reports that more than 500 children die each year and more than 3,500 are injured in unintentional shootings. The *Dallas Morning News* reports that fourteen American children are killed by guns every day. The National Center for Health Statistics puts the number of young people between the ages of fifteen and nineteen killed by firearms each year at more than 4,000, counting both intentional and unintentional shootings. According to the Centers for Disease Control and Prevention, more teenagers die of gunshot wounds than of all natural diseases combined.

In 1994 the firearms industry sold $670 million worth of new handguns.

An article published in the *Journal of the American Medical Association* suggests that a partial solution to the problem of child injury and death would be to equip firearms with trigger locks. These could be simple combination locks, magnetic locks that could be deactivated only by someone wearing a special ring, or locks that could be activated and deactivated by other technologies, none of which would significantly delay a gun owner in unlocking a gun. The NRA is, of course, opposed.

The idea that gun violence is a public health problem and that gun deaths and injuries can be prevented by reasonable measures is not new. The NRA, however, works to discredit research in this field—in fact, even to wipe out a federal agency that has done some research on it.

The National Center for Injury Prevention and Control is part of the federal Centers for Disease Control and Prevention in Atlanta. In 1995 the NRA mounted a campaign to cut the center's appropriation. Why? Because $2.4 million of the center's annual appropriation of $43 million goes toward research on firearms injuries. The center studies ways to reduce injuries from a variety of causes, including fires, falls, drowning, and firearms accidents.

An NRA spokesman complained about the center: "They want to foster a negative image against law-abiding gun owners. . . .

All [their] research comes to the conclusion that owning a gun is bad and dangerous to your health." The research is "obviously flawed," the NRA concluded.

Flawed? The *New England Journal of Medicine* and the *Journal of the American Medical Association* subject the articles they publish to peer review. Both have published articles from the National Center for Injury Prevention and Control. To this the NRA spokesman said, "We have a problem with those organizations, too, for not holding the articles to their usual standards."

More than 37,000 people died of gunshot wounds in 1992, including those occurring in homicides, suicides, and accidents. This is information the NRA doesn't want you to have. The NRA is so determined to keep it from you that it has added the National Center for Injury Prevention and Control to its growing list of enemies.

Of course, the NRA also demonizes the news media. The August 17, 1989, issue of *Time* magazine featured a cover story headlined "Death by Gun," in which it reported the number of people killed every year by firearms in crimes and accidents. How did the NRA react? Its Institute for Legislative Action issued an angry newsletter called *NRAction.* It said, on its front page, "Twenty-eight pages of this weekly magazine were devoted to advocate an anti-gun message and then attempt to pass it off as news! . . . TIME's purpose is transparent. It is a cheap way to sell magazines."

A year later the NRA mocked *Newsweek* for printing an article "rehashing homicide data."

Time and *Newsweek* are by no means the only news media attacked by the NRA for distributing "anti-gun" messages. Its special nemeses are the *New York Times,* the *Washington Post,* and the *Boston Globe.* These are, of course, "Eastern establishment" newspapers who can't possibly understand the attitudes of the good people of the South and the West. The television networks have come in for their share of NRA condemnation, especially Tom Brokaw of NBC.

To win NRA censure, you don't have to mention the NRA by name or say anything about pending legislation. All you have to do is suggest that guns do sometimes kill people. That's enough.

The official NRA line has always been that "Guns don't kill people. People kill people." Sure. But suggesting that the people who kill people very often use guns for the purpose will win you a picture in the NRA rogues' gallery.

A number of states have passed laws providing that a handgun owner is guilty of a crime if he or she has left a handgun improperly stored or secured and a child is killed or injured by that handgun.

One such law was enacted in Connecticut in 1990 after a boy was killed in Naugatuck. The police in Naugatuck charged the owner of the pistol that killed young D.J. Kenney with reckless endangerment for keeping a loaded and unsecured firearm in his house. The charge was dropped. Not long after that, D.J.'s mother, Susan, founded an organization she called GRIEF—Gun Responsibility in Every Family.

There are now chapters of GRIEF in many states and thousands of members. GRIEF did not ask that handguns be banned, only that the law require they be safely stored, that new guns have trigger locks, and that owners of guns not safely stored be charged with a felony if their guns caused death or injury. An eminently reasonable idea. Susan Kenney said, "I wasn't asking people to throw their guns away. Just to be careful."

How did the NRA react? When Susan Kenney arrived at Hartford for a legislative committee hearing, she was confronted by busloads of angry NRA members. The bill may have been reasonable, but they were vehemently unreasonable. They had their apocalyptic vision once again: that any gun control was the opening that would surely lead to the "disarming of America."

NRA representatives tried to gut the bill. They tried to amend out its only significant provisions; NRA representatives offered to help Susan Kenney get her bill passed if she would drop the trigger-lock provision and the provision making it a felony when an unsecured gun caused a child's death or injury. She refused to compromise. The bill passed.

Florida had passed such an act a little earlier. More states have enacted them, including New Jersey and Hawaii. The laws that GRIEF works for have nothing to do with banning guns, only with requiring that they be handled safely and responsibly.

To the NRA, such laws violate what they imagine is the mandate of the Second Amendment.

In recent years the NRA has sought to recruit women. It has run a series of ads showing women who "refuse to be a victim." The message of the ads, if they are to be believed, is that not only women in their homes, but also women in such places as parking garages, are safer if they carry a handgun.

The firearms industry has focused on women as a potential new market. FIE Corporation offers women its Titan Tigress, a gold-plated pistol that comes in a gold lamé purse. New Detonics offers a Ladies Escort Series of .45-caliber handguns, including purple pistols with gold-plated accents. Lorcin Engineering offers a chrome-plated pistol with pink grips. Smith & Wesson has instituted what it calls its LadySmith Program. It began running ads featuring .38-caliber revolvers "that manage to be elegant without sacrificing any of their practicality."

The opinion these manufacturers have about women would be comic if the subject were anything but deadly firearms.

The NRA, not surprisingly, is allied closely with the firearms manufacturers in promoting the idea that women should buy and learn to use handguns.

To a small extent, the campaign could be working. Women are buying guns, and they are going to firing ranges to learn to use them. But TV news snips showing women firing pistols at firing ranges may be another example of anecdotal evidence.

The National Opinion Research Center at the University of Chicago has found that the percentage of women who are gun owners stands at approximately 8 percent and has not changed significantly since 1980. The number of women applying for handgun permits in New York City has not increased much in the past few years. Colt and Smith & Wesson report that sales of their pistols designed for women are minuscule.

Twenty-six female members of Congress signed a letter to the NRA, protesting its "refuse to be a victim" campaign and asking that it be stopped. Representative Nita Lowey characterized the NRA campaign as an attempt by the NRA to get women to buy guns by "preying on their legitimate fears." Wayne LaPierre noted that gun purchases by women are growing rapidly and said "the market's being driven by fear."

The fact is that the NRA has probably just about saturated

the market in terms of recruiting more male members. The arms manufacturers may believe they have sold about as many guns to men as they are going to sell. According to Robert W. Hunnicutt, writing for *American Rifleman,* Smith & Wesson conducted a study that showed about 29 percent of men were interested in owning a gun, but about 28 percent of them already had a gun, whereas of the 19 percent of women interested in owning a gun, only 9 percent had one. The result was the Smith & Wesson LadySmith line of guns.

For the NRA, here is a whole new membership pool; for the gun manufacturers, a whole new market. For the manufacturers, it isn't working out that way. For the NRA, maybe.

Both the membership and gun-sales campaigns are based entirely on fear. Those fears are legitimate. Life in American cities has reached a saturation point with armed malcontents and opportunists. Dialing 911 will not save the average person on the street from muggers, rapists, robbers, burglars, carjackers, or murderers, nor can the judicial system stop crime with mandatory sentences, nor can politicians solve the problem with get-tough rhetoric.

But no matter how strident the propaganda from the NRA, the problem also will not be solved by arming every potential victim. Even if both predator and victim are armed, the victims are almost always untrained and taken by surprise. The predators will usually have the upper hand.

I am not concerned with the vision that obsesses the NRA—an America in which the citizens are slowly deprived of their weapons by the sinister machinations of a democracy that then transforms overnight into a military dictatorship. I do not see a time when we Americans will need our guns at home to stage a coup to reclaim our democracy.

What I see is a time, already here, when armed criminals rule the night in our major cities, a time when our government is too hogtied by the paranoid fears of the NRA and its ilk to safeguard the populace.

When reasonable limitations on gun sales are put into effect, they work. And we need not trammel on the Constitution to enact those reasonable limitations. The Brady Law has been a greater success than even its staunchest supporters had hoped.

State legislators are doing their part. South Carolina enacted a similar law after discovering that people were coming to South Carolina to buy cheap handguns and take them north, where they became the weapons used in criminal activity. South Carolina uses an instant background check of would-be gun purchasers. This has reduced the number of guns sold to felons. Also, the law has helped South Carolina capture fugitives from other states when they attempted to buy guns there.

For years Virginia, especially the environs around Washington, D.C., was gunrunners' heaven. People from the Northeast would drive to Virginia and buy five, ten, twenty or more guns, stash them in the trunks of their cars, and drive them to Pennsylvania, New Jersey, New York, Connecticut, Massachusetts, Rhode Island, and so on, where there were waiting periods, background checks, and, in the case of New York, an outright prohibition on handgun sales except to people with licenses. The profit was enormous, and the ready availability of guns in Virginia made a mockery of the gun ban just across the Potomac River in Washington, D.C.

Then Virginia governor Douglas Wilder secured passage in 1993 of a simple limitation—that no one person could buy more than one handgun a month in Virginia.

The results have been exactly what was intended. Although gun crimes have not diminished in the Northeast, a far smaller percentage of the guns seized by police after crimes are traceable to Virginia. Gunrunners can still drive to other southeastern states and load up with guns, but their most convenient source, Virginia, limits them to one a month.

The NRA fumes. Their chief lobbyist, Tanya Metaksa, says, "All it has had an effect on is making everybody worry if they buy a gun, can they buy another one within a thirty-day period? They're now deathly afraid that if they go try to buy a gun inadvertently because they didn't keep track of the days, they get caught into being a criminal unintentionally."

Hogwash. If NRA members have that much trouble keeping track of what day of the month it is, the magazine would do them a service by publishing a calendar and then getting out of the way of states like Virginia that want to stop the flow of deadly weapons to criminals.

The truth is that the NRA must kick up a stink about something, no matter how irrational, to justify its increasingly unwanted presence. In spite of insistence by Wayne LaPierre and Tanya Metaksa that all is well with the NRA, the organization is in serious trouble.

In the first six months of 1995, the NRA lost almost 10 percent of its membership. A May 1995 *Time*/CNN poll of gun owners shows that only 47 percent of them support NRA positions in general. This is down from 67 percent a few years ago.

The same poll shows that only 24 percent support the repeal of the assault-weapons ban.

Polls conducted by CBS, ABC, NBC, *USA Today, Time, Newsweek,* and the *New York Times* showed similar results. Although the NRA has growing influence with Congress, its extreme and uncompromising stands do not appeal at all to the public. In his "jack-booted thugs" letter, LaPierre dismissed these polls as "phony."

He knows they are not phony.

The American people are disgusted by the National Rifle Association. In the first half of 1995, more than 323,000 members of the NRA were so disgusted that they did not renew their memberships.

Handgun Control, Inc., is the NRA's true Satan. Just about anything it says drives NRA hard-liners into spluttering fury. Richard Aborn, president of Handgun Control, makes a cogent point when he says the NRA "may be on the verge of marginalization. It's going to get weaker if it continues to delude itself."

It looks as though the NRA leadership is bent on destroying the organization. Indeed, many of its former leaders say that is exactly what is happening: that the NRA is self-destructing, alienating the public by its intransigence and spending itself into bankruptcy all in the name of preserving its take on the Constitution.

If anything in this debate is phony, it is the claim of the NRA to be the guardian of the Constitution. It is anything but.

EPILOGUE

Within the NRA's cloistered walls, the shoot-to-kill crowd keep a stubborn finger on the trigger. The moderates, who can't seem to get organized, seem limited unhappily to hand-wringing in the backrooms.

In the fading weeks of 1995, the front man, Thomas Washington, passed away and was succeeded by a front woman, Marion Hammer, as president. That's "Hammer" as in the pistol part that strikes the firing pin; for she is a pistol-packing grandmama who fired her first gun at age five.

She quickly moved up to the firing line alongside Tanya Metaksa. The two women, both in their fifties, have drawn "a line in the sand," to quote Hammer, and dare anyone with political ambitions to cross it.

APPENDICES

APPENDIX A

CONGRESSIONAL GUN CREW

In this book, I have identified the NRA as Public Enemy No. 1. But who are its accomplices? Who're the hit men and women who do the NRA's bidding on Capitol Hill? I have compiled a blacklist for the edification of the electorate. It's based on an exhaustive search of the records.

THE BIG GUNS

Here are members of Congress who have received the biggest contributions from the NRA. Some have already earned their campaign cash. Others, who are new to Congress, can be expected to do so:

Senator Bill Frist (R) Tennessee	$187,127
Senator Fred Thompson (R) Tennessee	$182,177
Senator James Inhofe (R) Oklahoma	$ 99,900
Senator Paul Coverdell (R) Georgia	$ 95,806
Senator Richard J. Santorum(R) Pennsylvania	$ 91,175
Congressman George Nethercutt (R) Washington	$ 79,725
Congressman Harold Volkmer (D) Missouri	$ 51,046
Congressman Pat Danner (D) Missouri	$ 45,706
Congressman Don Young (R) Alaska	$ 41,696
Senator Conrad Burns (R) Montana	$ 36,877
Congressman Bart Stupak (D) Michigan	$ 32,152
Congressman Bill Brewster (D) Oklahoma	$ 30,103
Congressman R. Cunningham (R) California	$ 29,990

Congressman Stephen Buyer (R) Indiana	$ 29,880
Congressman Gerald Solomon (R) New York	$ 29,700
Congressman James Quillen (R) Tennessee	$ 29,700
Congressman John Doolittle (R) California	$ 29,590
Congressman Mike Parker (D) Mississippi	$ 28,414
Congressman Bill Zeliff (R) New Hampshire	$ 26,482
Congressman Alan Mollohan (D) West Virginia	$ 25,750
Congressman Dan Burton (R) Indiana	$ 25,240
Congressman Nick Rahall (D) West Virginia	$ 25,000
Congressman Earl Hilliard (D) Alabama	$ 24,750
Congressman Charles Taylor (R) North Carolina	$ 24,750
Congressman Gary Franks (R) Connecticut	$ 24,750
Congressman Charles Wilson (D) Texas	$ 24,300
Congressman Ike Skelton (D) Missouri	$ 23,261
Congressman Mark Neumann (R) Wisconsin	$ 23,253
Congressman Frank LoBiondi (R) New Jersey	$ 23,072
Congressman Toby Roth (R) Wisconsin	$ 22,800
Congressman Donald Manzullo (R) Illinois	$ 22,008
Congressman Rick Boucher (D) Virginia	$ 21,800
Congressman James Talent (R) Missouri	$ 21,636
Congressman Newt Gingrich (R) Georgia	$ 21,607
Congressman Bill Emerson (R) Missouri	$ 21,350
Congressman B. Vucanovich (R) Nevada	$ 21,100
Congressman Jim Lightfoot (R) Iowa	$ 20,850
Congressman Roscoe Bartlett (R) Maryland	$ 20,800
Congresswoman Kay Bailey Hutchinson (R) Texas	$ 20,459
Congressman Scott McInnis (R) Colorado	$ 20,115

APPENDIX B

THE NRA HIT MEN

The following men and women have voted pro-NRA after receiving generous campaign contributions by the gun lobby. We have broken the list down and listed the culprits by state and their voting records. We have also listed any monies they received and the dollar amount.

SENATE

The following have voted against all major gun control issues (1985–1994). The dollar amount is that which the NRA has given in support of the candidate since 1989/1990.

Alabama		**Idaho**	
Richard Shelby (R)	$10,226	Larry Craig (R)	$13,286
		Dirk Kempthorne (R)	$ 9,900
Alaska			
Ted Stevens (R)	$11,197	**Iowa**	
Frank Murkowski (R)	$ 9,900	Charles Grassley (R)	$ 9,900
Arizona		**Kentucky**	
John McCain (R)	$ 9,900	Mitch McConnell (R)	$ 8,035
Florida		**Mississippi**	
Connie Mack, III (R)	$ 4,950	Trent Lott (R)	$ 9,900
		Thad Cochran (R)	$ 4,950
Georgia			
Paul Coverdell (R)	$95,806	**Montana**	
		Conrad Burns (R)	$36,877

New Hampshire
Robert C. Smith (R) $11,000
Judd Gregg (R) $ 5,950

North Carolina
Launch Faircloth (R) $17,973
Jesse Helms (R) $17,957

Oklahoma
Don Nickles (R) $ 9,900

South Dakota
Larry Pressler (R) $15,400

Texas
Phil Gramm (R) $ 9,900

Utah
Robert F. Bennett (R) $ 9,900
Orrin G. Hatch (R) $ 4,950

Wyoming
Alan K. Simpson (R) $ 0

The following voted against all major gun control issues all but once (1985-1994). The dollar amount is that which the NRA has given in support of the candidate since 1989/1990.

Colorado
Hank Brown (R) $ 0

Missouri
Christopher Bond (R) $ 0

New Mexico
Pete Domenici (R) $ 4,950

Texas
Kay Bailey Hutchinson (R) $20,459

The following voted against major gun control issues all but twice (1985-1994). The dollar amount is that which the NRA has given in support of the candidate since 1989/1990.

Alabama
Howell T. Heflin (D) $15,194

Kansas
Bob Dole (R) $ 4,950

Louisiana
J. Bennett Johnston (D) $ 9,508

Pennsylvania
Arlen Specter (R) $16,146

CONGRESS

The following voted against all major gun control issues (1986-1994). The dollar amount is that which the NRA has given in support of the candidate since 1989/1990.

Alaska
Don Young (R) $41,696

Alabama
Spencer Bachus (R) $ 5,950
Terry Everett (R) $ 3,000

Arkansas
Tim Hutchison (R) $ 6,450
Jay Dickey (R)   —*
*The NRA paid $17,381 fighting against Dickey in the last election.

Arizona
Bob Stump (R) $11,490

California
R. Cunningham (R) $29,990
John Doolittle (R) $29,590
Duncan Hunter (R) $16,740
Richard Pombo (R) $15,328
Ken Calvert (R) $15,165
Jerry Lewis (R) $14,400
Carlos Moorhead (R) $ 1,500
David Dreier (R) $ 2,000
Jay Kim (R) $ 2,000

Colorado
Scott McInnis (R) $20,115
Wayne Allard (R) $16,215
Dan Schaefer (R) $ 9,950

Florida
John Mica (R) $11,900
Karen Thurman (D) $ 7,450

Georgia
Newt Gingrich (R) $21,607
John Linder (R) $17,350
Mac Collins (R) $ 9,900
Jack Kingston (R) $ 4,950

Idaho
Michael Crapo (R) $15,850

Illinois
Donald Manzullo (R) $22,008
Tom Ewing (R) $ 5,000
Dennis Hastert (R) $ 3,646
Phil Crane (R) $ 2,485

Indiana
Stephen Buyer (R)	$29,880
Dan Burton (R)	$25,240
John Myers (R)	$12,635

Iowa
Jim Lightfoot (R)	$20,850

Kansas
Pat Roberts (R)	$12,900

Kentucky
Ron Lewis (R)	$14,850
Jim Bunning (R)	$ 0

Louisiana
Jim McCrery (R)	$ 7,250
Richard Baker (R)	$ 6,324
James Hayes (D)	$ 5,950
Billy Tauzin (R)	$ 4,500
Bob Livingston (R)	$ 3,700

Maryland
Roscoe Bartlett (R)	$20,800

Michigan
Bart Stupak (D)	$32,152
James Barcia (D)	$ 9,900
Dave Camp (R)	$ 8,950
Joe Knollenberg (R)	$ 6,950
Vernon Ehlers (R)	$ 0

Minnesota
Collin Peterson (D)	$ 9,900

Mississippi
Mike Parker (D)	$28,414
Gene Taylor (D)	$17,615

Missouri
Harold Volkmer (D)	$51,046
Pat Danner (D)	$45,706
Ike Skelton (D)	$23,261
Bill Emerson (R)	$21,350
Mel Hancock (R)	$17,718

Nebraska
Bill Barrett (R)	$ 8,850

Nevada
B. Vucanovich (R)	$21,100

New Mexico
Joe Skeen (R)	$11,600

New York
Gerald Solomon (R)	$29,700
Bill Paxon (R)	$17,850
John McHugh (R)	$10,900

North Carolina
Howard Coble (R)	$ 4,050
Cass Ballenger (R)	$ 3,868

Ohio

John Boehner (R)	$ 6,290
Paul Gillmor (R)	$ 3,300
Martin Hoke (R)	$ 290

Oklahoma

Bill Brewster (D)	$30,103
Frank Lucas (R)	$13,400
Ernest Istook (R)	$ 8,450

Oregon

Wes Cooley (R)	$ 1,000

Pennsylvania

George Gekas (R)	$ 3,115
Robert Walker (R)	$ 2,300

South Carolina

Floyd Spence (R)	$ 4,900
Bob Inglis (R)	$ 0

Tennessee

James Quillen (R)	$29,700
John Tanner (D)	$ 5,750

Texas

Jack Fields (R)	$18,350
Henry Bonilla (R)	$14,850
Frank Tejeda (D)	$14,850
Pete Geren (D)	$13,217
Sam Johnson (R)	$11,249
Tom DeLay (R)	$ 9,550
Joe Barton (R)	$ 9,187
Lamar Smith (R)	$ 6,100
Larry Combest (R)	$ 5,650
Dick Armey (R)	$ 3,500
Bill Archer (R)	$ 0

Utah

James Hansen (R)	$16,565

Virginia

Rick Boucher (D)	$21,800
Lewis Payne (D)	$14,065
Robert Goodlatte (R)	$12,400
Norman Sisisky (D)	$ 7,815
Tom Bliley (R)	$ 3,000

Washington

Jennifer Dunn (R)	$ 0

West Virginia

Alan Mollohan (D)	$25,750
Nick Rahall (D)	$25,000
Robert Wise (D)	$13,215

Wisconsin

Toby Roth (R)	$22,800
Steve Gunderson (R)	$ 9,900

The following voted against all major gun control issues except when they were absent for voting (1986-1994). The dollar amount is that which the NRA has given in support of the candidate since 1989/1990.

Alabama
H.L. Callahan (R) $ 2,600

California
Wally Herger (R) $ 3,650

Kentucky
Hal Rogers (R) $ 9,900

Pennsylvania
Bud Shuster (R) $10,900

Texas
Charles Wilson (D) $24,300

The following voted against all major gun control issues all but once (1986-1994). The dollar amount is that which the NRA has given in support of the candidate since 1989/1990.

Alabama
Earl Hilliard (D) $24,750
Tom Bevill (D) $ 1,500
Glenn Browder (D) $ 1,300

Arizona
John Shadegg (R) $ 5,500

California
Edward Royce (R) $14,850
Bob Dornan (R) $12,190
D. Rohrabacher (R) $10,540
Howard McKeon (R) $10,215
Bill Baker (R) $ 5,614

Colorado
Joel Hefley (R) $ 5,115

Florida
Charles Canady (R) $10,215
Tillie Fowler (R) $ 0
Bill McCollum (R) $ 0

Michigan
Peter Hoekstra (R) $ 0

Mississippi
G.V. Montgomery (D) $ 7,500

Missouri		Ron Klink (D)	$ 5,450
James Talent (R)	$21,636	John Martha (R)	$ 0

New Hampshire
Bill Zeliff (R) — $26,482

Tennessee
John Duncan (R) — $ 5,900

North Carolina
Charles Taylor (R) — $24,750

Texas
Greg Laughlin (R) — $19,390
E. De la Garza (D) — $12,829
Solomon Ortiz (D) — $10,400
Ralph Hall (D) — $ 6,450

Ohio
David Hobson (R) — $ 2,390
Rob Postman (R) — $ 0

Utah
Bill Orton (D) — $11,900

Pennsylvania
Tim Holden (R) — $18,850
Bill Clinger (R) — $ 8,025

The following voted against all major gun control issues all but twice (1986-1994). The dollar amount is that which the NRA has given in support of the candidate since 1989/1990.

Alabama
Bud Cramer (D) — $ 8,000

Florida
Cliff Stearns (R) — $ 6,468

Arizona
Jim Kolbe (R) — $ 5,290

Georgia
Nathan Deal (D) — $ 7,450

California
Christopher Cox (R) — $10,350
Ron Packard (R) — $ 3,000

Illinois
Jerry Costello (D) — $ 6,100
Glenn Poshard (D) — $ 0

Connecticut
Gary Franks (R) — $24,750

Iowa
Jim Nussle (R) — $11,400

Michigan		**Pennsylvania**	
Nick Smith (R)	$ 0	Paul Kanjorski (D)	$11,400
Minnesota		**Virginia**	
James Oberstar (D)	$ 5,500	Owen Pickett (D)	$ 2,000
New Mexico		**Wisconsin**	
Steve Schiff (R)	$18,100	Tom Petri (D)	$11,550

Sources for Appendices

Campaign donation amounts taken from the 1989–1994 reports of the Federal Elections Commission.

Senate voting records represent the eighteen NRA-related votes that occurred between 1985–1994 as compiled by Handgun Control, Inc.

House of Representative voting records represent the seventeen NRA-related votes that occurred between 1986–1994 as compiled by Handgun Control, Inc.

INDEX